For the World's Best GOLFER

First published in Great Britain in 2010 by

Prion Books
an imprint of the
Carlton Publishing Group
20 Mortimer Street
London W1T 3JW

A catalogue record for this book is available from the British Library

ISBN 978-1-85375-767-9

Printed in the UK by CPI Mackays, Chatham, ME5 8TD

^{For} the World's Best
GOLFER

*A Full Round of Fun for
the Expert on the Course*

Mike Haskins and Clive Whichelow

PRION

CONTENTS

Introduction

What's the difference between you and Tiger Woods? Apart, of course, from a slight gap between your handicaps, and perhaps a small variance in the cost of your golf clubs, and possibly a piffling disparity between your respective bank balances?

Well, he plays golf for a living and you play it for enjoyment. In your own mind you probably have no doubt at all that if you could just get rid of your boring day job for a while and spend a bit more time on the golf course you could be up there with Tiger, Phil, Steve, Lee and Paul and the rest of them.

In fact, you're sure of it. You've probably even given some of the golfing greats the benefit of your personal tuition from time to time. Not that they've listened of course. They were on the TV at some distant course at the time while you were dispensing your expert advice from the comfort of your armchair. 'No, Tiger, not the 2-iron!', 'Phil, Phil, Phil, you need to play to the left of the green!' But on they went regardless. They may even have won their matches but perhaps they could have had an even better win if only they'd listened to you.

No, all modesty aside, you know you're good don't you? If only you had that little bit more time to devote to the game, perhaps a tad more encouragement from your partner ('Surely you're not playing golf this weekend are you? It's our Julie's wedding day....') Oh, they just don't understand do they?

A lucky break would be nice too. You see these people on TV talent shows who are working in a supermarket one minute then playing Vegas the next. That talent didn't just appear overnight; they had it all along, just waiting to be discovered. That's what they need – a golf talent show! They could call it the G Factor. You'd probably win it outright. But then you'd end up as a professional golfer. Doing it for a living. Another day, another dollar. Clocking on at tee time, clocking off when the light began to fade. Where would be the fun in that?

No, you're probably better off as you are; playing for the sheer delight of seeing that little white ball soaring majestically over the fairway in a perfectly defined arc and plop – straight into the water; playing for the heroic satisfaction of finally chipping the ball out of the bunker on the fifteenth attempt; playing week in, week out knowing, just knowing, that one day you will achieve the ultimate – a hole-in-one. Ok, it may not necessarily have been the hole you were aiming for, and if it is you may have to spend several hundred pounds of your hard-earned cash buying everyone in the bar a drink, but hey, that's golf. No one ever said it was going to be all fun.

And when the assembled throng raise their glasses at the nineteenth hole, casting admiring glances in your direction, and with tears of joy trickling down their sand-spattered cheeks, there will be only one appropriate toast: 'For the world's best golfer!' Enjoy.

TEEING OFF

Mainwaring: I've been trying to get in the golf club for years.
Wilson: Yes, well, they are rather particular, sir.

Dad's Army

Golf is...

Golf is a lot of walking, broken up by disappointment and bad arithmetic.

Anon

Golf is a game whose aim is to hit a very small ball into an even smaller hole, with weapons singularly ill-designed for the purpose.

Attributed to Winston Churchill

Golf is a game in which one endeavours to control a ball with implements ill adapted for the purpose.

Attributed to Woodrow Wilson

Golf is an open exhibition of overweening ambition, courage deflated by stupidity, skill scoured by a whiff of arrogance.

Alistair Cooke

Golf is not a sport. Golf is men in ugly pants, walking.

Rosie O'Donnell

Golf is a game where white men can dress up as black pimps and get away with it.

Robin Williams

Golf is a science, the study of a lifetime, in which you can exhaust yourself but never your subject.

David Forgan

Golf is played by twenty million mature American men whose wives think they're out having fun.

Jim Bishop

Golf is a game that needlessly prolongs the lives of some of our most useless citizens.

Bob Hope

First lesson

Archie goes to his local golf club for his first lesson with the pro
and begins by explaining that he knows nothing whatever about
the game. The pro shows him the stance and swing and says,
'Now just hit the ball toward the flag on the first green.' Archie
tees up and smacks the ball straight down the fairway and onto
the green, where it stops inches from the hole. 'Now what?'
Archie asks the speechless pro. 'Er,' says the pro, 'now you're
supposed to hit the ball into the hole.' 'Oh for goodness sake!'
splutters Archie in disgust. 'NOW you tell me!'

Beginners' questions answered

Q. What is the difference between a bogey and a birdie?
A. A bogey is the sheer bad luck a golfer experiences when going
   one over par. A birdie is the consummate skill displayed by a
   golfer in going one under par.

Q. Why is a two under par shot known as an eagle?
A. Because you're never likely to see one, let alone have one.

Q. What club should I use to get out of a high tree?
A. Probably the local parachutists' club.

Q. If I get a hole-in-one do I have to buy all the drinks?
A. If you start saving now you'll probably have enough to buy
   the whole country a drink by the time you get a hole-in-one.

Q. What does it cost to join a golf club?
A. Your time, your sanity, and maybe even your marriage.

The lesson you really need

George and Hugo play every Sunday and every Sunday George thrashes Hugo and wins money from him, so Hugo decides to have some lessons. He pays out several hundred pounds over a few weeks but can still never manage to beat George. After a year Hugo has paid out several thousand pounds and is still no closer to beating George.

'I don't get it,' says Hugo, 'How do you always manage to beat me? I've spent a small fortune on golf lessons. Have you been having golf lessons too?'

'No,' says George, 'I haven't had a single golfing lesson. But I've found this really good bloke who's helped me brush up on my cheating.'

Alternative golf lessons

Golf lessons are usually about stance, grip, swing and all that sort of stuff, but what you don't learn are some of the other finer points of the game. So, here, free of charge are a few alternative tips for golfers everywhere.

1. Don't beat the boss. If you go off for a round with the man who decides your salary increases it's not a good idea to totally humiliate him on the golf course. He may be rubbish and you may be the reincarnation of Bobby Jones, but don't. Do. It.

2. Learn from your mistakes. This may mean that you are going to be learning one heck of a lot, but if you want 'easy' become a Sunday footballer.

3. Trust nobody. He may be your best friend. He may have even been best man at your wedding. You trust him with your most intimate secrets, but for gawd's sake don't trust his scoring.

4. Learn the irregular verb of cheating: he cheats, they cheat, I am lucky.

5. Your expenditure on golf equipment should be inversely proportional to your handicap. You just don't need a £500 club to triple bogey.

6. Don't think that just because you have put some money on the outcome of your game that you will suddenly play better. You won't.

7. There is no such thing as an unmissable putt. Make your opponent play every single one.

8. Invent your own golfing lingo. Most players will know about whiffers, mulligans and condors, but if you tell your opponent he has just played a 'Marley' or a 'parakeet' he may be sufficiently impressed to take your word on the finer points of the rules.

9. Don't try to teach golf to anyone else. If they're bad they'll blame you and if they get good they'll beat you. You literally can't win!

10. Get yourself a nickname. All the best golfers have nicknames and it will make you seem more glamorous and professional. They're easy to think up, too. If your surname is Jones you become 'Jonesy', if your surname is Smith you become 'Smithie'. Don't do it though if your surname is Monk, Wall or Doubleboge.

11. Don't fear hazardous courses. They give you far more excuses when everything goes pear-shaped.

12. Don't use monogrammed golf balls. It will be a source of embarrassment for years to come as they are fished out of lakes, coughed up by family pets, or found in roads surrounding your local golf course.

13. Develop a sense of humour about your golfing abilities. You're going to need it.

14. Remember, there is no such thing as luck in golf. There is skill, and there is bad luck. Unless of course we're talking about your opponent.

How do you spell that?

A young woman is taking her first ever golfing lesson. 'Tell me,' she asks her instructor, 'is the word spelt p-u-t or p-u-t-t?' 'P-u-t-t is correct," he replies. "To put' means to place a thing where you want it while 'to putt' means a vain attempt to do the same thing.'

It's like learning to play golf. Just when you think you've cracked it, they move the goalposts.

Adrian Love

The lessons are how much?!

Object: to hit a ball into a hole. Why would you need lessons? How hard can it be?

Like most games, it's all very simple in theory, but the reality can often be a bit trickier. Maybe that's how young kids sometimes get holes in one – perhaps they are unencumbered by too many thoughts of technique. But many people have lessons and they don't always come cheap. It is said that the world's most expensive golf lesson will set you back $1,500. That's for three whole hours though, and you can get a full day for just $3,000. And if you take lessons with Mitchell Spearman you're following in the spiked footsteps of pros such as Greg Norman and Nick Faldo.

No one who ever had lessons would have a swing like mine.

Lee Trevino

An inexperienced player

A woman is accompanying her husband on a round of golf. At the first stroke he hits the ball in the rough. She shakes her head in sympathy. On the second stroke he hits the ball into a bunker. She shakes her head and sighs. On the third stroke the man knocks the ball on the green and it rolls into the hole. 'Oh boy,' says his wife. 'Now you're in real trouble.'

World's biggest golf lesson

According to *Guinness World Records*, the most participants to take part in a single golf lesson is 389. Colin Montgomerie gave the assembled multitude their lesson at the Army Golf Club, Aldershot, Hampshire on February 16, 1999.

Well, at least somebody's learnt something

A novice lady golfer is at the golf course swiping at her ball and sending earth flying in all directions. 'My goodness,' she remarks to her caddie, 'the worms will think there's an earthquake.' 'I don't know about that,' replies the caddie. 'The worms round here are quite clever. At the moment they're probably all hiding underneath your ball for safety.'

Golf is so popular simply because it is the best game in the world at which to be bad...

A.A. Milne

The ultimate in golf lessons

In 2002 the University of Birmingham became the first in the UK to offer a BA in golf. Over 100 people applied for the course, but only 26got in. But it won't be endless rounds of golf for students. They have to study everything from business management to the workings of muscle groups in the human body to the biomechanics of a golf ball in flight. The course was set up as a joint venture between the university and the Professional Golfers' Association (PGA). Just imagine the faces of parents though when they ask their children what their plans are when they leave school: 'Well, Mum, I'm going to spend three years on a golf course....'

Doctor's orders

Dave is extremely nervous and neurotic and works in a very stressful job. He has been to the doctor several times 'for his nerves' and has been given a succession of pills. None of them have worked very well, so he goes back to the doctor and asks what else he can do for him.

'Do you play golf?' asks the doctor.

'No,' says Dave.

'Well we've tried everything else. Why not give it a try?'

The first time Dave goes out on the golf course, he hits the ball into the woods on the very first shot and spends 45 fruitless minutes looking for it before coming out with nothing more than a lot of nettle stings. He then hits the ball into the sand and spends another frustrating ten minutes trying to chip it onto the green. On his third hole he knocks the ball into the water hazard. By the end of his first day he is a nervous wreck and goes back to the doctor to tell him so.

'Keep it up for another month,' advises the doctor. And so Dave spends day after day playing hopeless shots and getting more and more frustrated and agitated.

At the end of the month he goes back to the doctor with his nerves in shreds and begs him to give him something to calm him down.

'Well, Dave,' says the doctor, 'I think I've already tried you with every pill on the market. 'How did you find the golf by the way?'

'That's made me ten times worse!' complains Dave. 'Why on earth did you recommend this stupid game to calm my nerves?!'

'Oh, it wasn't to calm your nerves,' replies the doctor. 'It was to make you realize that however bad you think things are, you should just thank the Lord you're not a golfer as well!'

Golf is...

Golf is an awkward set of bodily contortions designed to produce a graceful result.

Tommy Armour

Golf is a game in which the ball lies poorly and the players well.

Art Rosenbaum

Golf is an ideal diversion but a ruinous disease.

B.C. Forbes

FROM THE SCOTTISH MISTS OF TIME
Early rounds

Golf may have started with ancient shepherds passing the time by knocking rocks around with their crooks. There is some evidence that shepherds' implements were used in games with rocks. In 1338, German shepherds were granted special dispensation to mark their territories by striking a pebble with their crooks. The distance covered was the extent of their grazing rights. Not only that but their sheep must have helped keep the grass nice and short on these early courses!

Some have argued that golf developed from the ancient Roman game of paganica which involved hitting a wool or feather stuffed leather ball with a bent stick. There was also an English game called cambucca in which a wooden ball was hit with a curved club and in France there was a game called jeu de mail in which a wooden ball was hit down a 'fairway'.

And that's before we even get to the medieval Dutch game, Spel Metten Kolve.

Yes! Kolf! Geddit!

In fact Spel Metten Kolve literally means 'game with clubs'. This involved hitting a ball over long distances and even over icy canals. Well, there probably wasn't much choice in Holland was there?

On 26th December 1297, the townsfolk of Loenen aan de Vecht in northern Holland commemorated the relief of the Kronenburg Castle one year earlier. They did this by playing four 'holes' of Spel Metten Kolve.

Historians have however dismissed the claims that jeu de mail or spel metten kolve were the forerunners of golf as there was an essential ingredient missing from both games. And that missing essential ingredient was, ironically, a hole!

One of the earliest images of what appears to be golf is in a sketch of the Great East Window of Gloucester Cathedral which is believed to date from 1340. The window featured scenes from the Battle of Crecy in France and appeared to show a man in the process of striking a ball as though in a game of golf. The game being played is however probably not golf as we would know it. It would be the old English game cambucca or the Flemish game of chole.

You're doing really well

A novice golfer goes for his first lesson with a golf coach and spends a couple of hours practising his stance, his swing, his concentration, his grip, his mental attitude, and many other aspects of the game. At the end of his two hour session, he asks the coach how he's done.

'Fantastic!' says the coach, taking his £75 fee. 'In fact, you've done so well, I think that next time we might start using a ball!'

Golf banned!

King James II attempted to ban golf in Scotland in March 1457. He was concerned that his men were wasting time that should have been spent on archery practice. He gave out an edict that declared that 'futebaw and golf be utterly cryt done and not usyt'. Instead the men were ordered to spend their time on archery ranges. Notice that even in 1457 James II's Scottish accent was quite apparent in his spelling of the word 'futebaw' (i.e. football).

After James II's reign, the ban was reaffirmed in 1470 and

1491. Unfortunately many people chose to ignore the king's edict. This would have been bad enough but among those ignoring the king's edict was the king himself!

James IV thought golf was a 'ridiculous sport' but nevertheless was talked into having a go in 1502. He was of course soon hooked. The king employed a bowmaker in Perth to make him a set of clubs, he bought himself some special golfing clothes and spent an entire February one year doing nothing except hunting and playing golf.

So what with the failure to get the young men of Scotland practicing their archery skills, could the allure of golf have spelt the beginning of the end of the country's status as a military power?

Sunday golfers?

When golf on the links was banned on Sundays to stop people skipping church some enterprising souls started playing the game in the churchyards. Because of the obvious hazards involved the holes necessarily had to be shorter and were usually between 50 and 100 yards.

Columbus went around the world in 1492. That isn't a lot of strokes when you consider the course.

Lee Trevino

Mary, Queen of Clubs

Mary Queen of Scots (1542–87) was the first woman to play golf in Scotland. Her enthusiasm for the game was so great that it caused a scandal and she may even have lost her life partly as a result of her love of golf.

At the age of five Mary was sent to live in France. While at the French court Mary enjoyed playing golf as one of her favourite activities and is therefore credited with helping to spread the popularity of the game.

Mary played in France with French military students or cadets who were forced to carry her clubs. And that is believed to be the origin of the term caddie.

When she was 15, Mary was married to the French king's son, Francis. In a good move Francis succeeded to the French throne in 1559 but then in a slightly less good move one year later, he caught an ear infection. The ear infection developed into a brain abscess and this in turn developed into death. And so by 1560 Mary was no longer Queen of France and had to return to Scotland.

Mary got married for a second time to Henry Stuart aka Lord Darnley. The marriage was not a success to say the least and ended with Darnley's murder in rather suspicious circumstances. The house that Darnley was staying in exploded and he was found lying outside having been strangled.

This did not however seem to put Mary off her golf! The Earl of Moray later testified that, rather spending a proper time in mourning, he had seen Mary playing golf just a few days after Darnley's murder. Mary was suspected of involvement in the murder and being spotted having a quick round of golf a few days afterwards didn't help her cause.

Mary spent most of the remainder of her life in imprisonment. She was eventually tried for treasonous activities against the English throne and beheaded at Fotheringay Castle in Northamptonshire in February 1587.

There was good news for golfing fans though! Mary and Darnley's son was crowned King James VI of Scotland and he went on to become not only James I of England but a keen golfer too!

Golf was originally restricted to wealthy, overweight middle-class businessmen; today it's open to anybody with hideous clothing.

Dave Barry

Mason about on the golf course

In the late 18th and early 19th century golf ceased to be a Court game enjoyed by the British royal family. George III, William IV and Queen Victoria were not interested in the game. Furthermore it is argued that golf might have died out as a popular pastime around this time had it not been for the enthusiasm and organization of one particular group of people: the Freemasons.

The members of early golf clubs were Freemasons and it is said to be thanks to the communication network between lodges that the first rules of golf were circulated.

So perhaps when Masons give each other their famous secret handshake, what they are in fact doing is showing off the way they hold their golf clubs!

The influence of the Masons also helped spread the love of golf around the world through various outposts of the British Empire. A golf club was founded in Calcutta in 1839 and another in Bombay in 1842. In that same year New South Wales got its first golf club while Montreal had to wait until 1873.

Perhaps most significantly it was a mason who took golf to America. David Deas, originally from Leith in Scotland was the first Provincial Grand Master Mason in what were then the American colonies and in 1743 ordered 96 golf clubs and 432 balls to be sent over. Deas' Charleston Club might have a claim to be one of the world's oldest golf clubs but unfortunately its minutes were lost.

Indeed William St Clair, 19th Baron of Rosslyn, who founded the world's acknowledged first golf club in 1744 and laid the foundation stone of the world's first golf club house had also been the first elected Grand Master of the Grand Lodge of Scotland in 1736. St Clair was the last male heir of the Rosslyn branch of the St Clairs, died in 1778 and was buried in Rosslyn Chapel.

The Masons! Rosslyn Chapel! Sinclair! The Da Vinci Code isn't going to turn out to be all about golf is it?

———

'The Honourable Commissary and Magistrates of Fort Orange and the village of Bererwyck, having heard divers (diverse) complaints from burghers of this place against the practice of playing golf along the streets, which causes great damage to the windows of the houses, and also exposes people to the danger of being injured and is contrary to the freedom of the public streets; therefore their honours, wishing to prevent the same, hereby forbid all persons to play golf in the streets, under the penalty of forfeiture of Fl. 25 for each person who shall be found doing so.'

Dutch ordinance at Fort Orange
(later Albany, New York) 1659

Those Chinese invented everything!

The Chinese Nationalist Golf Association claims golf is of Chinese origin. The Chinese game of Ch'ui wan is referred to in records written by Wei Tai of the Song Dynasty in 943 AD. In Chinese, chui means hitting and wan means small ball. According to the theory this game was brought to Europe in the 12th and 13th centuries by Mongolians. And according to experts the rules of Ch'ui wan are remarkably similar to those of modern day golf.

'To the GOLF PLAYERS

The Season for this pleasant and healthy Exercise now advancing, Gentleman may be furnished with excellent CLUBS and the veritable Caledonian BALLS, by enquiring at the Printer's.'

Advertisement for golfing equipment in Rivingston's Royal Gazette, *a New York newspaper, in 1779*

The first pro

Allan Robertson (1815 – 1859) was a feather golf ball and club maker who is regarded by many as the game's first professional player. Robertson came from a family of golf ball makers in St Andrews whose lineage could be traced back to 1610 when their ancestor Thomas Buddo was a ball-maker in St Andrews. He was the first man to break 80 in 1853 on what is now the Old Course at St Andrews.

Old Tom and young Tom

Old and Young Tom Morris were two of the greatest golfers of the 19th century. Old Tom Morris was the father of Young Tom Morris who proved to be even more of a golfing genius than his father. With sad irony Old Tom did indeed live to the good old age of 86 while Young Tom died young aged just 24.

Old Tom was born in 1821. He was apprenticed as a club and ball maker to Allan Robertson. The pair fell out when Morris broke a promise he had made not to use the new gutta percha golf balls that appeared from 1848 and which Robertson had been attempting to suppress because of the threat they posed to his feather ball making business.

Old Tom helped design many golf courses including Prestwick, Royal Dornoch, Muirfield, Carnoustie, Royal County Down, Nairn and Cruden Bay. His golf design services were charged at £1 per day plus expenses. He also standardized the length of courses to 18 holes.

In 1860 in the first Open Championship at Prestwick, Morris was runner-up to Willie Park who beat him by two shots. The canny Scotsman may have known what he was doing though. The runner-up was paid £3 while the champion just had to make do with the honour of being named 'Champion Golfer' of the year.

Old Tom went on to win the Open in 1861, 1862, 1864 and 1867. His 1867 win at the age of 46 set a record which survives to this day for the oldest person to win the Open. In 1862 Morris had also set a record for the largest margin of victory (13 strokes) in a major championship. This was only broken at the 2000 US Open by Tiger Woods with 15 strokes.

Young Tom also won the Open four times. The first of these was in 1868 when Young Tom really was young – just 17! It was also at this event that Young Tom scored the first ever hole-in-one at the championship. Young Tom won again in 1869 when Old Tom was runner-up, an achievement so far unmatched by any other father and son.

Following Young Tom's third successive win in 1870, he was given the Open Championship belt to keep. Young Tom's first round score in 1870 of 47 over 12 holes, has never been equalled or bettered. There was no Open in 1871 so Young Tom's win in 1872 was his fourth successive victory. He was awarded prize money of £8.

Tragedy however struck soon after. Young Tom had married Margaret Drinnen, a miner's daughter who had already borne a child out of wedlock. At the time this was of course considered scandalous and Old Tom did not attend Young Tom's wedding. In September 1875 Young Tom received a telegram telling him that his pregnant wife had suddenly become very ill. Both she and the baby died leaving Young Tom broken hearted. He died three month later on Christmas Day 1875 aged just 24 years old.

Old Tom carried on playing in the Open Championships until 1895 when he was 74. He died in 1908 a few weeks after fracturing his skull as a result of falling down the stairs at the St Andrews clubhouse.

Golfing USA

In 1887 New Yorker Robert Lockhart was going on a business trip to Scotland. His friend, John Reid, asked him to bring back six clubs and balls. Lockhart could not resist trying the equipment straight away on his return and hit a few shots on the frozen Hudson River before delivering the consignment to Reid. Reid laid out a three-hole course in a cow pasture in Yonkers and in November 1888 the St Andrews Golf Club was founded, the oldest surviving golf club in America.

By 1895, there were over 50 clubs, and by the turn of the century, more than 900, with at least one club in each state. By 1930, this had grown to over 5,000 courses being enjoyed by 2,125,000 players and 800,000 caddies.

At first however golf was considered an effete sport by many Americans. But then in 1913, Francis Ouimet won the US Open defeating two British stars and golf became increasingly accepted by the general American public.

Golf combines two favourite American pastimes: taking long walks and hitting things with a stick.

P.J. O'Rourke

Amateur good, professional bad

The word 'amateur' often carries with it negative connotations, but it wasn't always so. In the early part of the twentieth century many clubs in the UK treated the amateurs better than the professionals. Professionals would be brought into clubs to coach wealthy amateur players but were not granted permission to use all the club's facilities, and were not even allowed to enter the clubhouse through the front door, but had to go in at the back of the building – the 'tradesman's entrance'.

When the American golfing legend Walter Hagen came over to England to take part in the 1920 Open he was refused permission to enter the clubhouse by the main entrance. So he chose not to enter the clubhouse at all and asked for champagne to be brought out to his limousine which was parked outside. The club members were not amused.

Bobby Jones, one of the greatest ever golfers, kept his amateur status throughout his golfing career, as did many other golfers of his era.

A 112-year wait

In 2016 sporting history will be made when golf returns to the Olympics after an absence of 112 years. The game was included in the second modern Olympics in Paris in 1900, and again in St Louis in 1904, but since then it has not been an Olympic sport.

One of the arguments against it being included is that it is already a high-profile sport with several major events at which to compete, but the same could be said for other sports. In its favour it has been pointed out that at the Olympics players could compete as individuals and not as part of a team as in other international golf events.

At the 1900 Olympics the gold and silver medals were won by Britons Walter Rutherford and David Robertson respectively. At St Louis in 1904 gold was won by Canadian George Lyon, and silver by American Chandler Egan.

While golf will be included in the 2016 Olympics, spare a thought for those sports that tried but failed to be included: baseball, karate, softball, squash, and roller sports.

GOING ON A COURSE

During an interview with Jack Nicklaus, the interviewer effusively said, 'Jack, you are amazing, your name is synonymous with the game of golf. You really know your way around the course. What is your secret?' Jack said simply, 'The holes are numbered.'

Eighteen holes

Why 18 holes? Why not 20, or 12, or 100? Well, at one time the number of holes did vary from course to course. Before 1764, for example, the old course at St Andrews had 22 holes while others might have had as many as 25 or as few as 4. But by 1858, St Andrews had decreed that a golf course should consist of 18 holes and it has remained at that figure ever since. No one knows exactly why it was decided to settle on the figure of 18, though one source suggests that, perhaps in keeping with the game's Scottish roots, the number of holes had to tally with the number of measures in a bottle of whiskey. Shot for shot as it were.

There are approximately 31,857 golf courses in the world. This means that if you played one course every day, it would take you about 87 years to get round all of them!

Musselburgh Links

In March 2009 Musselburgh Links in East Lothian, Scotland was recognized by *Guinness World Records* as the oldest golf course in the world.

According to the official world record pronouncement:

'The Musselburgh Links, The Old Golf Course in Musselburgh, Scotland, UK, is the oldest golf course in the world. Documentary evidence proves that golf was played on Musselburgh Links as early as 2 March 1672, although Mary Queen of Scots reputedly played here in 1567.'

The record was validated by entries in the Account Book of Sir John Foulis of Ravelston, including one dated March, 1672.

Originally Musselburgh had just 7 holes although this was increased to 8 in 1838 and 9 in 1870. This was then deemed quite enough and Musselburgh has remained a 9 hole course ever since although this does restrict its appeal to new members.

It has been estimated that in the USA golf courses cover an area about 1,550 square miles. If all the USA's golf courses were combined they would therefore cover an area larger than the state of Rhode Island.

How many holes are we supposed to have again?

In 1744 when the Honourable Company of Edinburgh Golfers held their first contest, Leith Links had 5 holes.

Blackheath also had 5 holes but, like Leith, eventually added 2 more.

Bruntsfield Links similarly had 5 holes at this time, but had only room to expand to 6.

Montrose Links went from 7 holes by 1810, 14 in 1825, 11 in 1849 and a lavish 25 in 1866.

In 1764 St Andrews Old Course had 12 holes, 10 of which were played twice making 22 holes in all.

In 1764, the first four holes were combined into two, making 10 in all, 8 of which were played twice producing a satisfying round of 18. And of course over time, this has become the standard number of holes for courses all around the world.

Floyd Satterlee Rood played golf right across the United States from September 14, 1963, to October 3, 1964. He did the 3,397.7 mile trail in 114,737 strokes and lost 3,511 balls along the way.

You can't move
here for golf courses

Golf Digest identified the following countries as having the highest density of courses (based on countries with a minimum 500,000 population):

Singapore (one course every 10 square miles)

England (one every 27 square miles)

Northern Ireland (every 40 square miles)

Wales (every 50 square miles)

Scotland (every 56 square miles)

Japan (every 59 square miles)

The Netherlands (every 75 square miles)

Mauritius (every 87 square miles)

Republic of Ireland (every 95 square miles)

Denmark (every 117 square miles)

In total approximately 0.014 per cent of the Earth's land mass is devoted to golf courses!

The course veteran

A young avid golfer is trying to squeeze in a quick round one afternoon when an old gentleman shuffles onto the tee and asks if he could accompany him as they are both golfing alone. The young man agrees and is surprised to discover that his aged companion plays fairly quickly without wasting much time. On the 9th fairway however, the young man is faced with a tough shot when he finds a large pine tree standing directly between his ball and the green. The old man steps up and advises him, 'When I was your age, I'd hit the ball right over that tree.' The young golfer can't resist rising to this challenge, so he swings hard, hits the ball up into the top of the tree trunk and watches it drop back down and land about a foot from where it began. The old man steps up again and tells him, 'Of course, when I was your age that pine tree was only about three feet tall.'

A world record was set at Tatnuck Country Club, Worcester, Massachusetts on September 9, 1996. A team led by Joy Wetzel and Flip Davis completed an 18-hole round of golf in 9 minutes and 28 seconds. Presumably the hourly charge for use of the greens must be a bit steep over there!

Somewhere on a golf course far far away...

Alan Shepard (1923–98) was the Apollo astronaut who played golf on the Moon. He was the commander of Apollo 14 on its mission to the Moon between January 31 and February 9, 1971 and was the fifth man to walk on the Moon.

According to NASA, 'Just before departure from the Moon on Apollo 14 mission, Alan B. Shepard drove a golf ball on the lunar surface.'

He had adapted the device used by astronauts for taking samples from the Moon's surface and fitted it with a No. 6 iron golf club head.

Speaking from the lunar surface Shepard told Mission Control, 'Houston... you might recognize what I have in my hand as the handle for the contingency sample return; it just so happens to have a genuine six iron on the bottom of it. In my left hand, I have a little white pellet that's familiar to millions of Americans. I'll drop it down. Unfortunately, the suit is so stiff, I can't do this with two hands, but I'm going to try a little sand-trap shot here.'

NASA reported that 'The one-sixth gravity on the Moon compensated for the difficulty Shepard had making a good swing in his bulky space suit and back pack.' According to Shepard his shot went 'miles and miles and miles'. Or possibly a couple of hundred yards.

To date Shepard remains the only person ever to have played golf on the Moon.

Honestly! Some men just have to take their clubs with them no matter what sort of trip they're going on!

We've got more
golf courses than you!

Which country in the world has the most golf courses per capita?
Why, none other than little old Scotland, according to research
by *Golf Digest* magazine in 2005. Perhaps it's fitting that what is
widely regarded as the home of golf should top the list.

But which country is second? Surely, it must be the USA, home
of so many golfing greats: Arnold Palmer, Jack Nicklaus, Sam
Snead, Lee Trevino, Tiger Woods....

No, in fact, the USA comes eighth on the list, behind countries
such as the Republic of Ireland (4th), Northern Ireland (5th)
and Wales (7th). So where are all the golfing greats from those
countries? There have of course been some: Ian Woosnam from
Wales, Padraig Harrington and Paul McGinley from Ireland, and
Sandy Lyle and Colin Montgomerie from Scotland for example.
But it's a case of simple arithmetic – a country of over 300 million
people (USA) is likely to produce more golfers than a country
of under 3 million (Wales). And where did England come on the
list? Tenth, just behind Sweden, and we have produced at least
a couple of household name golfers in the shape of Tony Jacklin
and Nick Faldo.

THE WORLD'S STRANGEST GOLF COURSES

Golf is tough enough, but some people like that little extra challenge such as playing in extreme temperatures, playing next to a volcano or maybe having to take a boat out to a floating hole. There's certainly no shortage of fabulous excuses should your game not go well. 'The ball was taken off by a bear', 'I would have won but for the frostbite that kicked in on the 15th', 'How was I to know the volcano was about to erupt?', 'Have you tried playing a ball out of the teeth of a crocodile?'

Yes, if you like to live dangerously there is no shortage of amazing, and quite frankly scary, places to play.

This should teach you to place your ball more accurately

There is a golf course at Camp Bonifas in Panmunjom on the border between North and South Korea. The course comprises just a single par 3 192 yard hole.

The course has a peeling Astro-turf green but what makes it truly unique is what lies around it, because this course is surrounded on three sides by minefields.

It was dubbed by Sports Illustrated magazine as 'the most dangerous hole in golf' and at least one errant shot is known to have detonated a land mine.

Camp Bonifas is therefore probably unlikely to host any major championships in the near future although it could be a destination for those wanting to try a golfing variation on Russian roulette.

Way off down the course

Chester arrives home one evening and his wife asks him how his golf game went. 'Well,' says Chester. 'I was hitting OK, but recently I've noticed my eyesight seems to be getting a bit worse. In fact to be honest after I took each shot, I couldn't see where the ball had gone.' 'Oh dear,' says Chester's wife before piping up. 'I've got an idea! Why not take my dad along with you?' 'But he's 85!' says Chester. 'He may be 85,' says Chester's good lady wife, 'but he's still got perfect eyesight.' So the next day Chester tees off with his wife's father looking on. Chester takes his swing and sends the ball way off down the middle of the fairway. 'So,' Chester asks his father-in-law. 'Did you see it?' 'Yes I certainly did,' comes the reply. 'So,' asks Chester, 'where did it go?' 'Where did what go?' says the old man.

That's rough

One day at the golf course Angus is having a bit of difficulty with his game. He turns to his caddie and says, 'This green is terrible. This has to be the worst golf course I've ever played on in my life.' 'What do you mean "course"?' says his caddie. 'You left the course about an hour ago!'

If you lose your ball in here you'll need extra strong gloves to pick it out

The Merapi Golf Course in Indonesia boasts breathtaking views. At 9,800 feet high Mount Merapi itself is particularly breathtaking, even more so if it happens to be erupting at the time.

Yes, the Merapi Golf Course is one of the very few courses in the world where play is conducted next to an enormous active volcano ready to blow at any moment. In 2006 massive clouds of ash and searing hot gas clouds came rolling down Merapi's slopes forcing a suspension of play due to volcanic eruption.

The 6,969 yard course is par 72 although you'll be particularly lucky to make this if you happen to land your ball in the volcano itself.

Course architects have not however so far designed a flag enormous enough to pop into Mount Merapi's massive bubbling crater.

Hawaii boasts the even more tell-it-like-it-is Volcano Golf Course which sits on the rim of the Kilauea volcano in Hawaii. And, yes, again it is active. So you takes your shots and you takes your chances. Oh, and isn't it slightly worrying that the name of the volcano sounds a bit like 'kill all o' yah'?

High tees

At 4,000 feet the Volcano Golf Course is pretty high, but if you want to go to the highest on Earth then you need to head to South America.

At 14,335 feet above sea level at its lowest point, Tuctu Golf Club in Morococha, Peru was famed as the highest golf course in the world. It has however now been abandoned although one wonders how many people who went there ever came back...

La Paz Golf Club in Bolivia is an 18 hole course 10,800 feet above sea level. Jade Dragon Snow Mountain Golf Course in Yunnan Province, China is at an elevation of 10,000 feet, while in the USA Copper Creek Golf Club, Copper Mountain, Colorado is at 9,700 feet. Yak golf course in Kupup, East Sikkim, India however stands at 13,025 feet above sea level. Don't forget though that failing to acclimatize to such heights can result in headaches, nausea, oedema and even death. And that's before you even tee off!

The world's hottest and coolest golfers

If you play golf at the Alice Springs course you may have to endure temperatures of up to 50 (yes, 50) degrees Celsius which, converted into Fahrenheit, is bloody hot.

Of course if extreme heat is not your thing, and you find you can't get a decent grip when your hands are covered in sun lotion then you could always try the North Star course in Alaska.

It's America's northernmost course and as well being able to chill out (literally, with temperatures sometimes in the minus twenties) you may be able to spot local wildlife such as perhaps a moose or maybe even a lynx.

Wildlife on the course

And if you don't mind encountering some even larger wildlife during your game you could head down to the Hans Merensky course in South Africa where you might bump into a giraffe or a zebra, or some other exotic species. They also have hippos, which could add an interesting dimension to the water hazards.

Elsewhere the official tourist website for Bangladesh outlines the attractions and potential dangers of some of the country's golf courses:

> *'Monu Valley Golf Club often adds a bit of 'excitement' to your round of golf. Situated amidst rubber groves, banyan trees and quiet paddies, you may be fortunate enough to have a Bengal tiger cross the fairways whilst you look on.*
>
> *Soi Dao Highlands golf course is another unique course. Elephants, deer and wild boar are protected in the area.'*

So be careful in case you start a herd of elephants stampeding when you shout 'Fore!'

If your ball lands within a club length of a rattlesnake you are allowed to move the ball.

Local rule at Glen Canyon Golf Club in Arizona

Australian meteorologist, Nils Lied, managed a drive of 2,640 yards at Mawson Base, Antarctica, in 1962. That's nearly one and a half miles. The ball travelled so far thanks to the Antarctic wind and the area's somewhat slippery playing surface!

That's not just your opponent snapping at your heels

The Lost City Golf Course in Sun City in South Africa is an 18 hole par 72 desert style golf course with views across the bushveld. It is said to be one of Gary Player's favourite courses.

If however you lose your ball in the water hazard adjacent to the 13th hole do not be tempted to step in to try and retrieve it. The Lost City course is one of the very few in the world to boast its own resident population of 38 crocodiles. The water trap at the 13th is said to be a graveyard for hundreds of sliced shots although hopefully not a graveyard for hundreds of half chewed golfers.

The club advises players not to fish balls out of the water. Actually chaps, we weren't going to.

But remember, if you see a pair of jaws opening towards you, you should be able to quickly prop them open with a 6 iron.

If a ball comes to rest in dangerous proximity to a hippopotamus or crocodile, another ball may be dropped at a safe distance, no nearer the hole, without penalty.

Local rule at Nyanza Golf Club, Uganda

Desert golf

Yes, you've probably been tempted to give up at some point – desert golf, that is – and go and take up something easier instead like blindfolded hang-gliding. But no, we're talking about desert golf. Golf in deserts. Did you know there's even a Desert Golf magazine?

Yes, Americans like their golf, and they're not going to let a few thousand square miles of desert stop them playing. Build it and they will come seems to be the Field of Dreams style motto of golfers out in places like Arizona and Nevada.

But judging by the pictures on the desertgolfer.com website we're not talking bleak and barren wastes of sand with the odd buffalo skull reminding players that they'd better be careful out there. No, it's verdant, lush and lovely, and believe it or not you may still encounter a water hazard or two. A water hazard in a desert? Come on, you're not going to get an easy ride wherever you play this game are you? You've been playing long enough to know that.

Please watch where you're swinging that thing

Established in 1993, La Jenny Golf Course in France is the only naturist golf course in Europe. La Jenny itself is a naturist village lying on the Atlantic Ocean. As well as its 10-hectare naked golf course, La Jenny also offers canoeing, horse-riding, cycling and archery. What could possibly go wrong?

———

Have you ever wondered if paediatricians take Wednesdays off to play miniature golf?

Where's the green again?

You might find something closer to what the phrase 'desert golf' conjures up by going to Kabul Golf Club in Afghanistan. This nine-hole course doesn't have greens, it has what the club itself calls 'browns', which some observers have described as black, being a mixture of sand and oil. The oil is there to stop the sand blowing around.

There was an earlier club, dating back to 1967, but that closed in 1978, and this one opened up in 2004 in a new location. First there was the small matter of removing a few Soviet tanks and other detritus but the course is still being used today, the only golf course in Afghanistan. Needless to say there are no water hazards, but you may have to negotiate a bombed-out barracks or other obstacles. Fees though, are reasonable. It's just $15 for a round, and afterwards you can visit the pro shop and restaurant. Who would have thought it?

If the purpose of golf is purgatorial, nothing more needs to be said. But if the purpose is to entertain as well as instruct, then let us pause in the mad rush for hazards, more hazards and still more and fiercer hazards.

William Hemingway

I hope your golf buggy's fully charged

Nullarbor Links in Australia claims to be the world's longest golf course. And with its 18 holes covering a distance of 848 miles (1,365 km), there's probably few challengers for the title.

The course is so vast it is spread not only over two separate states but over two different time zones. You can tee off in Ceduna, South Australia and reach the 18th in Kalgoorlie, Western Australia perhaps seven days later. Along the way you may have to drive as much as 100 km between consecutive holes.

The idea is that the par 72 course stretches along the Eyre Highway with one hole in each participating town or roadhouse. The individual holes are named after different features of the outback landscape. For example Hole 1 is Oyster Beds, the 5th is Dingo's Den, the 6th is Border Kangaroo, the 8th is Watering Hole and the 13th is Sheep's Back. Slightly more confusingly Hole 12 is Skylab (because fragments of the NASA space station Skylab landed nearby in July 1979 prompting an apologetic phone call from President Jimmy Carter to the local motel) while the 7th is Nullarbor Nymph (in reference to another occasion when the locals got the attention of the world's press by concocting a tall story about a naked Sheila who ran wild with the kangaroos).

When playing Nullarbor Links you can expect to see kangaroos, dingos and even Southern Hairy Nosed Wombats. And at Dingo Den hole, there's a resident crow ready to steal any stray balls. Each player to complete the course is awarded a certificate.

But does all this make the Great Victoria Desert that lies up to the north of the course the biggest sand trap in the world?

The floating hole

Now if you think you have problems on a fixed hole; how about a floating hole? There's only one in the world and it's at the Coeur d'Alene course in the Rocky Mountains of North Idaho. To get to the 14th hole you travel by boat, or the Putter Boat shuttle as the club likes to call it. To add to the fun it's only a par three. Is this also the only hole in the world that is completely surrounded by a water hazard?

Actually, it's not, because down in Mexico at the Four Seasons Punta Mita club, in Bahia de Banderas there is a hole on a natural island. It is the only one of its kind in the world. It is also probably the only hole in the world to be numbered 3b. It's an optional hole in addition to the usual 18. The course was designed by Jack Nicklaus, and when you're waiting for your opponent to take his shot you can while away your time spotting whales in the nearby Pacific Ocean. Remember that car that James Bond drove which turned into a boat as it went into the water? Well, at high tide you need to ride in an amphibious vehicle to get to that island hole. It's golf Jim, but not as we know it!

In space no-one can
hear you shout 'Fore'!

Despite astronaut Alan Shepard hitting a golf ball on the Moon during the Apollo 14 mission in 1971, lunar golf has not so far caught on with anyone else.

Nevertheless Japanese company Shimizu Construction has drawn up blueprints for the development of a lunar golf course.

Shimizu's plans include the construction of condominiums on the Moon. Each condominium would consist of a cluster of inflatable egg-shaped dwellings four storeys high and which would include tennis courts as well as golf courses.

Golf in the after life

Nelson is an avid golfer who is so obsessed with the game that he cannot bear the thought that he will no longer be able to play after he has died. This thought terrifies him so much that he consults a spiritualist. Nelson asks the spiritualist if he could consult a recently departed golfing partner for him to try and find out if golf exists in heaven. The spiritualist goes into a trance, communes with the spirits and afterwards tells Nelson, 'Well, I've got good news for you and I've got bad news.' 'OK,' says Nelson, 'so what's the good news?' 'The good news,' says the spiritualist, 'is that heaven does indeed have its own golf course. It's a beautiful course with the most magnificent club house you could ever imagine.' 'Excellent,' says Nelson. 'So what's the bad news?' The spiritualist replies, 'They've already accepted you as a new member and you're booked in for a game next Tuesday.'

TOP TIPS

The happy hooker

On his honeymoon Benjy tells his new wife, 'Maisie, darling,
I have something to confess to you. I am completely addicted to
playing golf. During our married life together, you'll probably
never see me at the weekend and every holiday we take will
be to different golf courses.' Benjy,' says Maisie, 'I also have a
confession that I must make to you. I'm a hooker!' 'Oh,' says
Benjy, 'Well, I don't see why you think that's a problem. All you
need to do is keep your head down and your arm straight.'

They say practice makes perfect. Of course it doesn't. For the vast
majority of golfers it merely consolidates imperfection.

Golfing coach to pupil: You've just got one main problem. You're
standing close to the ball... after you've hit it!

Technique

The secret of golf is to turn three shots into two.

Bobby Jones

The right way to play golf is to go up and hit the bloody thing.

George Duncan

Golf is golf. You hit the ball, you go find it. Then you hit it again.

Lon Hinkle

Golf is not a game of great shots. It's a game of most accurate misses. The people who win make the smallest mistakes.

Gene Littler

The real reason your pro tells you to keep your head down is so you can't see him laughing.

Phyllis Diller

Take 9 strokes off your score. Skip the last hole.

Anon

Alternative tips for beginners

When you start playing golf you start hearing tips about how to play – from friends, book, instructors, DVDs, partners, experts, pros.... Everyone, it seems, knows more about golf than you do. So as soon as you take up this great game you immediately feel like a loser. Everyone is telling you where you're going wrong. Sooooo, what you need is a confidence booster or two. Here are a few tips that you won't hear anywhere else.

1. Most people make the mistake of playing their first game of golf with someone better than themselves: a friend who's been playing for years perhaps, or a golf instructor. Find someone who's rubbish. Perhaps one of your kids, or a niece, or your granny. You will win. You will feel good about yourself. You will feel good about your game. You may even feel so good that you start dispensing advice to your rubbish golfing partner. Before long you might even have your own instruction DVD out on the market.

2. Cheat. Golf is hard enough as it is without all those bunkers and trees and water hazards. Buy a book on magic and the art of distraction. Carry spare balls concealed in secret pockets. Have an accomplice who drops a ball on the green for you at opportune moments.

3. Learn to not care. Golf is only frustrating if you care about it. If you're not bothered it takes all the pressure off, and you know what? All of a sudden you're playing better golf. Not that you're supposed to care about that of course.

4. Start your own golf club and have alternative rules. Don't forget, all rules were made up by someone. Why shouldn't you make up your own? It will keep your opponents on their

toes if you suddenly tell them at the end of a game that it's the person who played the *most* strokes who is the winner – but only if it's a Tuesday.

5. Go to the bar before the game, not after. Your game will seem so much better, if only to you. It will also help you to observe tip number three.

6. Don't spend a fortune on equipment. If you're going to lose a lot of balls they may as well be cheap ones. If you're going attempt to bend your clubs in half or hit things with them in frustration it's probably best if they're not $5500 Maruman 2010 Majesty Prestigio Gold Premium irons.

7. Find something else to think about some of the time. Have you noticed that when businessmen get together they talk golf, and when golfers get together they talk business? That way it deflects everyone's attention away from what you're not yet very good at.

8. Golfer: So do you think my game is improving?
Caddie: Oh yes. You're missing the ball much closer than you used to.

9. Golfing legend Jack Nicklaus was once asked why he teed his ball so high above the ground. He thought about this for a moment before replying, 'Through years of experience I've found that air offers less resistance than dirt.'

The long arm of Bill Murray

Kevin McKinney, director of the Academy of Golf at Grand Cypress, recalled helping actor Bill Murray with his chip shots. Murray kept 'flipping his wrists in the follow-through'. As a result a gimmick used only for 'the direst cases' had to be employed. The shaft of a 9 iron was wrapped onto Murray's forearm with athletic tape making the club an extension of the actor's arm. This improved Murray's chipping immediately but during lunch the same day, he appeared in the club dining room with the 9 iron still fixed to his arm. 'He ordered a bowl of soup, which he ate with his right hand while carefully keeping his left arm vertical with the club pointed to the sky.'

On June 18, 1976, Steven Ward took 222 strokes to get round Pecos Course in Reeves County, Texas. He was three years old.

Words of wisdom

They say golf is like life, but don't believe them. Golf is more complicated than that.

Gardner Dickinson

If you think golf is relaxing, you're not playing it right.

Bob Hope

If you drink, don't drive. Don't even putt.

Dean Martin

Confidence, of course is an admirable asset to a golfer, but it should be an unspoken confidence. It is perilous to put it into speech. The gods of golf lie in wait to chasten the presumptuous.

P.G. Wodehouse

Never break your putter and your driver in the same round or you're dead.

Tommy Bolt

I never learned anything from a match that I won.

Bobby Jones

It takes hundreds of good golf shots to gain confidence, but only one bad one to lose it.

Jack Nicklaus

Golf balls are attracted to water as unerringly as the eye of a middle-aged man to a female bosom.

Michael Green (The Art of Coarse Golf)

A golf ball can stop in the fairway, rough, woods, bunker or lake. With five equally likely options, very few balls choose the fairway.

Jim Bishop

It won't help to tell yourself, 'Don't hit it in the water.' Your mind will only hear 'water'.

Bob Rotella

My favourite shots are the practice swing and the conceded putt. The rest can never be mastered.

Lord Robertson

'Play it as it lies' is one of the fundamental dictates of golf. The other is 'wear it if it clashes'.

Henry Beard

Few pleasures on earth match the feeling that comes from making a loud bodily function noise just as your opponent is about to putt.

Reverse every natural instinct and do the opposite of what you are inclined to do, and you will probably come very close to having a perfect golf swing.

Ben Hogan

My swing is so bad I look like a caveman killing his lunch.

Lee Trevino

There are two things you can do with your head down – play golf and pray.

Lee Trevino

The only time my prayers are never answered is on the golf course.

Billy Graham

It's good sportsmanship not to pick up lost balls while they are still rolling.

Mark Twain

Always room for improvement

Harris is coming out of the club house to drive home following a particularly poor game of golf, when a policeman stops him and asks, 'Did you just tee off on the 18th hole about 20 minutes ago?' 'Yes,' says Harris. 'Well,' says the policeman, 'did you happen to hook your ball so that it went over the trees and off the course?' 'Yes, I did,' says Harris. 'How did you know?' 'Sir,' says the policeman in a very serious tone, 'your ball just flew out onto the main road where it smashed into a lorry driver's windscreen. The lorry driver then lost control of his vehicle and ploughed into five other cars and a fire engine. The fire engine was on its way to a blaze in the town centre which has now spread and destroyed an entire shopping arcade. May I ask, sir, what you intend to do about this matter?' Harris thinks carefully before responding, 'I think in future maybe I should tighten my grip and lower my right thumb.'

BUT IT'S IN THE RULES!

The first chapter in the Rules of Golf is etiquette. Apparently everyone starts reading at chapter two.

Nick Mokelke

The first set rules of golf

Golf's original 13 rules were first written down in 1744 by The Honourable Company of Edinburgh Golfers as follows:

Articles & Laws in Playing at Golf.

1. You must Tee your Ball within a Club's length of the Hole.

2. Your Tee must be upon the Ground.

3. You are not to change the Ball which you Strike off the Tee.

4. You are not to remove Stones, Bones or any Break Club, for the sake of playing your Ball, Except upon the fair Green and that only within a Club's length of your Ball.

5. If your Ball comes among watter, or any wattery filth, you are at liberty to take out your Ball & bringing it behind the hazard and Teeing it, you may play it with any Club and allow your Adversary a Stroke for so getting out your Ball.

6. If your Balls be found any where touching one another, You are to lift the first Ball, till you play the last.

7. At Holling, you are to play your Ball honestly for the Hole, and not to play upon your Adversary's Ball, not lying in your way to the Hole.

8. If you should lose your Ball, by it's being taken up, or any other way, you are to go back to the Spot, where you struck last, & drop another Ball, And allow your adversary a Stroke for the misfortune.

9. No man at Holling his Ball, is to be allowed, to mark his way to the Hole with his Club, or anything else.

10. If a Ball be stopp'd by any Person, Horse, Dog or anything else, The Ball so stop'd must be play'd where it lyes.

11. If you draw your Club in Order to Strike, & proceed so far in the Stroke as to be bringing down your Club; If then, your Club shall break, in any way, it is to be Accounted a Stroke.

12. He whose Ball lyes farthest from the Hole is obliged to play first.

13. Neither Trench, Ditch or Dyke, made for the preservation of the Links, nor the Scholar's Holes, or the Soldier's Lines, Shall be accounted a Hazard; But the Ball is to be taken out teed and play'd with any Iron Club.

John Rattray, Capt

Golf is the only game in the world in which good knowledge of the rules can win a reputation for bad sportsmanship.

Patrick Campbell

So just who was this John Rattray?

In 1744 the Gentleman Golfers of Leith renamed themselves The Honourable Company of Edinburgh Golfers and founded the world's first true golf club. They talked the city fathers of Edinburgh into providing a silver trophy to be presented to the winner of a golf tournament at Leith Links. In preparation for the tournament the Honourable Company wrote down golf's first set of rules.

Edinburgh's city council agreed to provide the trophy on 7th March 1744 and on 2nd April 1744 the tournament was played. This was done over just five long holes rather than the 18 we know today.

The first winner of the tournament held at Leith Links was John Rattray (1707 – 1771) who was awarded the title of 'Captain of the Golf'.

It may seem slightly suspicious that the winner of the first tournament was also the person who put his signature beneath golf's first set of rules. It is unclear however whether Rattray signed off the rules in his capacity as Captain of Golf or because he was their author.

Rattray was an Edinburgh surgeon and a member of The Royal Company of Archers. And if you just check Rattray's dates again, you might notice that this gentleman surgeon and golfer was lucky to live and enjoy playing the game quite as long as he did.

In July 1745, just over a year after Rattray won the tournament at Leith Links, Charles Edward Stuart (that's Bonnie Prince Charlie to me and you) landed in Scotland.

Bonnie Prince Charlie arrived intent on raising a rebel army to help him stake his claim to the British throne. Two weeks after he landed he sent the Rattray family a letter inviting them to join his cause. John Rattray became a surgeon in the Jacobite army and ultimately personal surgeon to Bonnie Prince Charlie.

The rebel army advanced into England and reached as far as Derby before retreating. After the decisive defeat of the Jacobites at the Battle of Culloden Moor in 1746, Rattray was taken captive by the British army. Prospects for the former personal surgeon to Bonnie Prince Charlie did not look at all good. Rattray was personally informed by his guards, 'If anyone hangs, you shall!'

But wait a moment! Rattray was a golfing man!

Luckily Scotland's most senior judge Lord Forbes was one of Rattray's old golfing buddies! Forbes made a direct appeal on his behalf to the Duke of Cumberland who had led the brutal suppression of the Scottish rebels. Thanks to Forbes' intercession, Rattray was eventually released and returned to Edinburgh in 1747. He lived another 24 years and even went on to regain the Silver Club and the captaincy of The Honourable Company of Edinburgh Golfers in 1751.

So you see how useful it can be to make a few friends down at your local golf club!

The first golf club

Although, as mentioned elsewhere in this book, the Honourable Company of Edinburgh Golfers is probably the oldest golf club in the world, there is one other, earlier claim. The Royal Burgess Golfing Society of Edinburgh claims a start date of 1735, some nine years before the HCEG, though sadly there are no contemporary records to support the claim. The first mention of its date of origin were not recorded until the publication of a nineteenth century edition of the Edinburgh Almanac.
So, whatever the claims and counter claims one thing is indisputable: the first golf club in the world was in Edinburgh!

The uglier a man's legs are, the better he plays golf. It's almost
a law.

H.G. Wells

The R&A

The Royal and Ancient Golf Club of St Andrews is one of the
oldest golf clubs in the world.

The club dates back to the Society of St Andrews Golfers. In
May 1754 '22 Noblemen and Gentlemen of the Kingdom of Fife'
presented a silver club to be competed for over the links of St
Andrews.

They went on to declare that 'the Noblemen and Gentlemen
above named being admired of the Ancient and healthful
exercise of the Golf, and at the same time having the interest
and prosperity of the ancient city of St Andrews at heart, being
the Alma Mater of the Golf, did in the year of our Lord 1754
contribute for a Silver club having a St. Andrew engraved on the
head thereof to be played for on the Links of St. Andrews upon
the fourteenth day of May said year, and yearly in time coming
subject to the conditions and regulations following.'

They became officially Royal and Ancient in 1834 when King
William IV gave the society his patronage. The R&A became the
leading authority on the game of golf and in 1897 it codified its
laws and appointed the first Rules of Golf Committee.

The R&A has been organiser of The Amateur and Open
Championships since 1920 and has also acquired responsibility
for a further nine championships and international matches.
The R&A is also golf's governing body in all territories except
the USA and Mexico. The R&A accepted authority for
administration of the Rules in 1897 and, since 1952, has jointly

issued the Rules with the United States Golf Association.

Since 2004 the R&A has, although still based in St Andrews, existed as a separate entity from the Royal and Ancient Golf Club of St Andrews.

Do I have to know rules and all that crap? Then forget it!
John Daly (after being asked to join the Royal and Ancient Golf Club following his win in the 1995 British Open)

The official size for golf holes

Four and a quarter inches became the standard diameter for golf holes during the 19th century.

The reason for this particular, although apparently random, size is that 4 ¼ inches was the width of the implement that was used to cut the holes at Musselburgh Links, now officially recognized as the world's oldest golf course.

In 1893 the R & A (The Royal and Ancient Golf Club of St. Andrews) made 4 ¼ inches the mandatory size for holes as part of their efforts to standardize the rules of the game. The ancient hole cutter that had been developed and used at Musselburgh since 1829 is still in existence and is now on display at the club.

You can, legally, possibly hit and even kill a fellow golfer with a ball, and there will not be a lot of trouble because the other golfers will refuse to stop and be witnesses because they will want to keep playing.

Dave Barry

Let's have some more rules!

When the rules of golf were first laid down in 1744 there were just 13 of them. Today there are 34, which still doesn't sound very many but then each rule has subsections, and some of the subsections have sub-subsections. Every four years the Royal & Ancient and the United States Golf Association meet up to clarify and amend the rules where necessary. The R&A also publishes decisions based on specific enquiries. These decisions can lead into some unexpected, and almost philosophical areas.

Are you scared of loose impediments?

For example, is a spider an insect? Well for anyone who's ever seen the film Arachnophobia, or for zoologists, the answer is no, a spider is not an insect, it's an arachnid. But for golfing purposes the R&A has decreed that a spider is an insect, and there are rules regarding insects. Surely you didn't expect there to be separate rules for spiders did you? Don't be silly. An insect is, you see, what is termed a 'loose impediment'.

What's a 'loose impediment'? It's something that is in the

flipping way of your ball, and just happens to be a natural object. You can remove it without incurring a penalty – unless it's in a bunker. An obstruction, on the other hand, is something that's in the flipping way of your ball but is artificial. Obstructions are further classified into movable obstructions or non-movable obstructions.

A multiplicity of hazards

There are decisions on lateral water hazards (different, one supposes, from just ordinary water hazards), animal footprints, umbrella carriers, 'casual water' and various other things the unfortunate golfer may encounter, though none, it seems, on streakers, though in R&A terms a streaker would probably be what they would categorize as an 'outside agency'. It wouldn't sound quite the same in the news reports though would it? 'At St Andrew's today a 34-year-old outside agency stripped to her underwear and ran across the 18th green.' And if the 'outside agency' elected to park herself directly in front of the flag, would she be, as a 'natural object', a loose impediment or an obstruction? With the regularity with which streakers appear at golfing events perhaps it's time the R&A made a specific ruling on this.

It's all gone pear-shaped

What about a half-eaten pear then, you may ask? Well, it's lucky that you did, because the R&A has indeed ruled on the subject of half-eaten pears.

A pear, it has been conceded, is a natural object. Fine. No arguing with that. Therefore it is a loose impediment. Which kind of means it got there by natural means. We'll leave aside the possibility that your opponent deliberately chucked in front of your ball, because this is after all a gentleman's game, is it not? But what if there's no pear tree on the course? In the circumstances it's hardly a natural thing to find then is it? In its ruling the R&A said in effect that just because a pear has been semi-chomped and there is no pear tree nearby it 'does not alter the status of the pear.'

Sometimes though, a loose impediment can become an obstruction. How? The R&A gives a couple of examples. A log is a loose impediment, but if you put some legs on it and turn it into a bench, hey presto! It becomes an obstruction for which different rules apply. Similarly a piece of wood can magically turn from loose impediment to obstruction if it is made into a charcoal briquette. Handy stuff to know.

Birds and crabs

Every eventuality, it seems, has been covered by the R&A. Your ball lands in a bird's nest. Do you have to play the ball from the bird's nest? No, not according to rule 1-4/9. A land crab is in the way of your ball in the bunker. Is it a loose impediment? Yes. But, because it's in a bunker removing it would be a breach of rule 13, subsection 4.

If you call on God to improve the results of a shot while it is still in motion, you are using 'an outside agency' and subject to appropriate penalties under the rules of golf.

Henry Longhurst

Cheating rules OK!

The other interesting thing about rules is that until someone points out that you can't do something you may never have thought of it yourself in the first place.

Take rule 8-2b/1 for example. It's all to do with whether a caddie is allowed to stand in such a position that his shadow indicates to his boss the line of play to be used.

Well, would you have thought of that all by yourself? It's brilliant, it's sneaky, it's simple, and could very easily be defended as accidental, but don't try it, because it's against the rules. And that's official.

Another one you may not have thought about is strategically placing your golf bag as an impromptu wind-break while trying to execute a tricky putt in gale-force conditions (it's possible that this ruse was born from necessity in the wilder highlands of Scotland). But don't try this one either – it's been outlawed.

Mental rules

The rules also seem to teeter on the edges of Freudian anxieties. 'Mental interference' is an interesting phrase in the world of golf.

What is means is this: although your opponent's ball isn't actually physically in the way of your ball, it's close enough for it to be seen out of the corner of your eye while trying to take a shot which requires some considerable concentration. Can we move it? In the words of Barack Obama and Bob the Builder, 'Yes we can!'

As the R&A meets with the USGA every four years to review and possibly amend the rules where necessary, we may not have heard the last of some the more arcane decisions. Who knows, there may yet be rulings on half-eaten kebabs, lost ramblers, UFOs, squirrels, dead bodies, snowmen, robotic caddies, and yes, those pesky streakers. Who'd be a golfer?

One rule you probably won't have to worry about

Oh, and one last rule that you might be interested in. You're in a match and you've played your ball towards the green, but when you reach where you thought it had landed the ball isn't there. You search and search then give up, concede the hole and your opponent plays his ball. When he putts it into the hole, guess what's there? Yes, that's right, your original 'lost' ball. What's the ruling? Come on, what are the chances of that happening? You might just as well ask for the ruling on a UFO landing on the green.

Getting to grips with the rules

But if you find that interpreting the rules of golf can be difficult help is at hand. In fact, it's all so complicated that one enterprising chap by the name of Barry Rhodes has written a book entitled *999 Questions on the Rules of Golf*. Yes, 999 is quite a lot, but you get the impression that if it were not for the need for a catchy title the book might just have easily have been called *1014 Questions on the Rules of Golf*, or perhaps *1508 Questions…*

The laws of golf

Some people say golf is a game, some say it's a sport. They're both wrong. It's a cross between ritual humiliation and torture. And it's a little-known fact that there are certain laws governing golf which are completely immutable. It won't necessarily help you to know these rules, but at least you'll know why your game just isn't getting any better.

1. Golf balls are allergic to grass. Hit them and they'll immediately head for the water, or the sand, or the trees. Anywhere but that short sweet grass on the green.

2. When you play the greatest shot of your life no one will be looking. But if you just accidentally waft the ball with the swing of your club while practicing and make it wobble almost imperceptibly on the tee your opponent will probably have filmed it on his mobile.

3. Regardless of how often you play golf your game will not noticeably improve.

4. The more expensive the balls the more quickly you will lose them.

5. Whenever your golf goes through a particularly bad patch, don't worry – there will come a day when it is even worse.

6. Your best drives will always be followed by lousy putts.

7. You will be guaranteed to play the worst golf of your life as soon as you suggest betting a few quid on the outcome.

8. If you ever try to teach someone the game they will beat you.

9. Opponents never seem to know the finer points of the rules when they make a mistake but have an intimate and detailed knowledge of every one you break.

10. Golf clubs have the power of hypnosis. Every time you see them sitting in the hall they draw you in, they persuade you that you are a great golfer, that you must go out on the golf course again this weekend, and yes, you will be brilliant!

11. You know instinctively where professional golfers are going wrong when you watch them on TV but you have absolutely no idea where you are going wrong yourself.

12. Golf instruction videos and DVDs are absolutely invaluable – to the people selling them.

13. When you mis-hit a ball it will always go where you don't want it to. Balls never fluke themselves onto the green, let alone down the hole.

14. If there were a golf theory test you'd probably pass it – it's just the practical that you can't quite get to grips with.

GOLFING GREATS

I have seen men who have won a dozen or more tournaments, upon teeing off for their first USGA Open Championship, come close to vomiting. And golf is no easy game when you are trying to hole a downhill three-footer and throwing up at the same time.

Charles Price

Tiger cub

Tiger Woods' first appearance on television as a golfer was on *The Mike Douglas Show*, broadcast in the USA on October 6, 1978.

Yes, that's not a misprint. Tiger was indeed only born on December 30, 1975. So the fact that he made his TV debut less than three years later represented pretty good going.

Tiger appeared on the syndicated daytime talk show with his dad, Earl Woods. He toddled on carrying his little golfing bag and proceeded to demonstrate his golfing prowess before the show's host as well as comedy and golfing legend Bob Hope.

Also on the show that day were actor James Stewart and former *Bugsy Malone* child star, Scott Baio who was then aged 17 and presumably suddenly feeling quite old.

At ten months old, Tiger had watched his father hitting golf balls into the practice net in the garage of their bungalow in Cypress, California. Young Tiger immediately started to imitate his dad's swing.

Earl Dennison Woods was himself a keen sportsman. He had been a star baseball catcher at Kansas State University but at the time prejudice was still endemic, and the major baseball leagues were closed to black players. He became a Green Beret in 1960 and fought in Vietnam.

While organizing rest and recuperation for US troops in Thailand, Earl met his second wife Tida. Tida described herself as, 'half-Thai, one-quarter Chinese and one-quarter white'. Earl described himself as 'half-black, one-quarter American-Indian and one-quarter Chinese'.

This presumably means that their son is one quarter Thai, one quarter black, one quarter Chinese, one eighth white and one eighth American Indian.

Or perhaps he's just 100% Tiger.

When Tiger Woods signed a $100,000,000 endorsement deal with Nike the talk show host Jay Leno joked, 'This marks the first time Nike has paid anyone of Thai descent more than 11 cents an hour!'

So Tiger's not your real name then?

Lots of the golfing greats have had all sorts of nicknames, and Tiger Woods' nickname is so well known – and so commonly used without any sort of comment – that many people are probably not aware of his actual birth name.

Just for the record, and so that you won't get caught out at your next pub quiz, his original name (i.e. the one that he was given at birth) was Eldrick Tont Woods. During the Vietnam War, Eldrick's father had often fought alongside Colonel Vuong Dang Phong of the Vietnamese army. Earl Woods clearly thought much of the Colonel and his nickname, 'Tiger' and thus began calling his son 'Tiger'.

By the time young Eldrick had reached the age of 21 the name Tiger had stuck and Eldrick had it legally changed. Guess he'd earned his stripes by then.

More golfing nicknames

OK maybe you knew all about Tiger, but let's try you out on some other golfing nicknames. Do you know the nicknames of any of the following:

Jack Nicklaus, Gary Player, Arnold Palmer, Gene Sarazen, Sam Snead, Ernie Els, Greg Norman, Walter Hagen, Colin Montgomerie, Lee Trevino, Tom Watson, Phil Mickelson, Ben Hogan, Craig Stadler, Michelle Wie?

If you got more than seven out of the fourteen listed above you're a fully-fledged golf nut. If you got all fourteen, maybe you should be getting out more and practising your swing instead of learning golf trivia! But well done anyway. And for anyone who didn't get them all, here are the answers:

Jack Nicklaus was of course known as Ohio Fats. He came from Ohio and he was, well, a bit fat in the early days. There's hope for all you girth-challenged golfers out there yet!

Gary Player's rather cool nickname was The Black Knight because of his penchant for wearing black. Not sure how that nickname would have gone down in his native South Africa, but it didn't do him any harm did it? And no, that Deep Purple song wasn't about him.

Arnold Palmer was known as The King. Yes, all right there was some other bloke called Elvis who used the same nickname, but Arnie just might have got there first.

Gene Sarazen's nickname was The Squire owing to his elegant appearance and demeanour. But he had another name too. He

was actually born Eugenio Saraceni.

Sam Snead specialized in powerful long drives and therefore became known as Slammin' Sam, or Slammin' Sammy.

Ernie Els was known as The Big Easy. Why? Well, he's big (6 foot 3) and he makes the game look easy. Oh, and he has another name too. His first name is Theodore, and Ernest is his middle name.

Greg Norman was known as The Great White Shark. Some say because of his blond hair, though the real sharks inhabiting the waters round his native Australia are not known for their hirsuteness. The other reasons stated have been his size (6 feet) and his aggressive style of play.

Not all nickname are quite so inventive. Walter Hagen's nickname was The Haig and Colin Mongomerie's was Monty for obvious reasons, and Michelle Wie, perhaps inevitably became known as The Big Wiesy. And what of the others?

Lee Trevino became known as The Merry Mex for his Mexican ancestry and jovial demeanour, Tom Watson was dubbed Huckleberry Dillinger for his mixture of innocent looks combined with a killer instinct. Ben Hogan was nicknamed the Wee Ice Mon by Scottish fans when he played at Carnoustie in the Open, but also had the nicknames The Hawk, and Bantam Ben.

Phil Mickelson's nickname of Lefty seems obvious enough for someone who plays left-handed, but in everything other than golf Phil is right-handed. It must be very confusing for fans when he signs autographs!

And who is the Walrus? John Lennon sang 'I am the Walrus', then in a later song he said 'the Walrus was Paul', but in the world of golf, the Walrus is Craig Stadler. And with his heavy frame and impressive moustache who's going to argue with that?

The usual suspects

Take a look at any list of the greatest ever golfers and you'll find the same names cropping up again and again. There are a few variations of course, but there is a handful who will probably be on almost everyone's top ten list. Here are a few of them:

Jack Nicklaus
(USA b. January 21, 1940)

He not only appears in most people's top tens, he's more often than not at the very top of the list. Between 1962 and 1986 he won 18 Majors (six Masters, four US Opens, three Opens and five PGA championships). He started playing at the age of ten and turned professional in 1961. In 1962 he won the US open, beating Arnold Palmer. Not a bad start! In later years he turned his hand to golf course design and it has been estimated that 1% of all the golf courses in the world have been designed by him.

I think I fail just a bit less than everyone else.

Jack Nicklaus

Professional golf is the only sport where, if you win 20 percent of the time, you're the best.

Jack Nicklaus

Gary Player
(South Africa b. January 11, 1935)

Gary Player started playing golf at the age of 14 and turned professional at 17. He won nine majors (three Masters, three Opens, one US Open and two PGA Championships). He is the only player in the twentieth century to have won the British Open in three different decades.

Golf is a puzzle without an answer. I've played the game for 40 years and I still haven't the slightest idea how to play.

Gary Player

Ben Hogan
(USA 1912–1997)

He started as a caddie and played golf with fellow caddie Byron Nelson, himself later another big name in the sport. He turned professional at the age of 17 and went on to win nine majors (two Masters, one Open, four US Opens and two PGA championships).

His career was almost cut short in 1949 when a serious car accident left him with multiple injuries. In this accident he would have been killed by his car's steering column had he not thrown himself in front of his wife Valerie to protect her.

The three things I fear most in golf are lightning, Ben Hogan and a downhill putt.

Sam Snead

Tiger Woods
(USA b. December 12, 1973)

After beginning to play golf at the age of two and appearing on *The Mike Douglas Show* with Bob Hope, he won the Junior World Championships six times and was featured in *Golf Digest* magazine at the age of five. He turned professional at the age of 20 and has won 14 Majors (four Masters, three Opens, three US Opens and four PGA championships). It was predicted that he may have even eventually surpassed Jack Nicklaus's record of winning 18 majors, but this achievement may have been put off track by difficulties in his personal life in 2009 and what he described as his 'indefinite break from professional golf.' Though at the time of taking this 'indefinite break' he was just 33 years old and Jack Nicklaus won his 18th major at the age of 46, so who knows? According to *Forbes* magazine he was the highest earning sportsman in the world in the year up to June 2009, having earned $110,000,000. Not only that, he was the highest earning sportsman in the world for the previous seven years too!

Fifty years ago, 100 white men chasing one black man across a field was called the Ku Klux Klan. Today it's called the PGA Tour.

Alex Hay

Gene Sarazen
(USA 1902–1999)

Sarazen started caddying at the age of ten and then began to play the game himself. He turned professional at the age of 18 and went on to win seven Majors (one Masters, one Open, two US Opens and three PGA Championships). His other great claim to fame, one which golfers around the world probably give thanks for regularly, is that he was the inventor of the sand-wedge. He started using this in 1932 at the British Open and went on to win the tournament. His original club is still on display at the Prince's Golf Club where the 1932 Open was held. And, appropriately enough, the Prince's Golf Club displaying the original sand wedge is at Sandwich in Kent.

Gene Sarazen tears the ball through the wind as if it did not exist.

Bernard Darwin

And now your starter for ten: what do the five players just mentioned have in common? Answer: They are the only five players in the history of golf to have won all four of the Majors (Masters, Open, US Open and PGA Championship), otherwise known as the Career Grand Slam.

Other players who regularly crop up on lists of all-time top ten golf players are Arnold Palmer, Sam Snead, Walter Hagen, Bobby Jones and Byron Nelson, and who knows, at some point in the future you might be on that illustrious list too.

Arnold Palmer
(USA b. September 10, 1929)

Arnold started playing golf at a young age as his father, Deacon, was head greenkeeper at the Latrobe Country Club in Pennsylvania. He didn't turn professional until he was 24, but went on to win seven Majors (four Masters, two Opens, and one US Open). Arnold Palmer also invented a drink, known understandably as the Arnold Palmer. It's made up of half lemonade and half unsweetened iced tea and is sometimes known as 'Arnold Palmer Tee' or a 'Winnie Palmer'.

Golf is deceptively simple and endlessly complicated.

Arnold Palmer

Sam Snead
(USA 1912–2002)

Another golfer who started as a boy caddie – at the age of just seven. He turned professional at the age of 22 and although he won seven Majors (three Masters, one Open and three PGA Championships) he never won the US Open. Though he did come second on his very first attempt in 1937. He is also probably the only professional golfer ever to have appeared in an episode of *Sgt. Bilko*.

Practice puts brains in your muscles.

Sam Snead

Walter Hagen
(USA 1892–1969)

He too started as a caddie and then went professional at the age of 20. He had been a very good baseball player and cancelled a trial with the Philadelphia Phillies in order to play a golf tournament. He won 11 Majors (four opens, two US Opens and five PGA Championships). He might have won a Masters or two, but they didn't begin until 1934 after his career had peaked. He was the first American to win the British Open, in 1922 (the 1921 winner, Jock Hutchinson became a US citizen in 1920 but as his name implies, he was born in Scotland).

Give me a man with big hands and big feet and no brains and I'll make a golfer out of him.

Walter Hagen

Byron Nelson
(USA 1912–2006)

He was caddying at the age of 12 and 8 years later was a professional golfer. He won five Majors (two Masters, one US Open and two PGA tournaments) but in 1945 he set a record that is still to be beaten: he won 11 tournaments in a row, and 18 altogether in that single year. To honour this extraordinary achievement the street where he lived in Roanoke, Texas has recently been renamed 'Eleven Straight Lane'. How cool is that?

The only shots you can be dead sure of are those you've had already.

Byron Nelson

Bobby Jones
(USA 1902–1971)

Probably the most extraordinary of the golfing greats, he won his first juniors' tournament at the age of six but never turned professional. He performed the amazing feat of winning what were then the four major tournaments of the Grand Slam (British

& US Opens, and British and US Amateur tournaments) all in the same year (1930), and not only in the same year, but within a period of four months!

He retired from golf at the age of 28. He also gained a BS in mechanical engineering and then a BA in English Literature from Harvard. He went to law school and was called to the bar after just a single year's study. Oh, and he also co-founded The Masters championship. He was also the only person ever to have two ticker-tape parades in New York City. To cap it all, he was only the second American to be granted the freedom of the City of St Andrews (in 1958). The first was Benjamin Franklin in 1759! When he died, play was suspended on the Old Course at St Andrews and the flag flown at half-mast. The 10th hole was named the Bobby Jones hole.

Golf is the only game I know of that actually becomes harder the longer you play it.

Bobby Jones

1912: Golf's *annus mirabilis*?

Three of the greatest golfers of all time were born within six months of one another in 1912. On February 4 out popped Byron Nelson, then on May 27 Sam Snead, and on August 13 Ben Hogan. Great for golf of course, but each of those players must at some time have thought when playing a tough match against one of their contemporaries: 'Why did those two have to come along at the same time as me?!'

Superstitions

Like many sportsmen, golfers often have their own little rituals, superstitions and beliefs that they think can affect their game.

Golfers often use coins as ball markers, but some American players will only use nickels, and others will insist on that nickel being heads up too. Paul Azinger went one stage further: he insisted on using a one cent coin (American penny) heads up with Abraham Lincoln facing the hole!

Some golfers are superstitious about what they wear too. Tiger Woods is said to like wearing red on Sundays, Lee Trevino used to favour black trousers and a red shirt on the last day of the tournament, and Gary Player liked to wear black.

The all-important balls too are a source of superstition. Sam Snead would only use balls with a zero on them, Hal Sutton preferred those with a number 2, and Dave Marr would only use number 3 balls. The numbers of course have no special significance (unless you're superstitious!) but are just there for identification purposes.

Arnold Palmer's wife, famously, used to kiss Arnie's golf balls before a match to bring him luck. This led to one of the most notorious commentator gaffes in the history of the sport:

That famous gaffe!

During a PGA golf tournament a TV commentator was talking about Arnold Palmer and a personal superstition that he'd heard the golfer observed. 'One of the reasons Arnie is playing so well,' said the commentator, 'is that before each tee shot, his wife takes out his balls and kisses them.' When the implications of this comment had sunk in the commentator suddenly exclaimed, 'Oh my God – what have I just said?!'

Even the tees can be lucky or unlucky. Jack Nicklaus liked to be given three white tees before a match, but Doug Sanders refused to use tees of that colour.

There may be something more than superstition in refusing white tees though. A similarity in the colour of the tee and the colour of the ball could be off-putting (no pun intended).

And finally, we come to a few superstitions that are shared by many golfers, professional and amateur.

The 13th hole is not a favourite of many players for obvious reasons. Changing balls while playing is considered unlucky by many, and starting after midday is a common no-no, though it's easy to see some logical reasons for these latter two superstitions.

Though whatever you believe brings you luck it's worth remembering what one golfer said when somebody commented on his luck. 'Yeah, I'm lucky; but you know what? The harder I practise the luckier I get.'

Great Golfers
ranked by height

It was once thought that there was some golfing advantage in being of small to average height. This was because many of the leading exponents of the sport once seemed to be around 5 foot 9 inches. According to one theory taller players might be at a disadvantage on a golf course because of their high centre of gravity which could cause problems on rough ground or in high winds. But then of course a taller player should have a greater swing which should theoretically mean he wouldn't have to be out so long tramping the rough ground and enduring the high winds.

Phil Blackmar	6 ft 7 in	Walter Hagen	5 ft 10.5in
George Archer	6 ft 5.5 in	Jack Nicklaus	5 ft 10 in
Ernie Els	6 ft 3 in	Arnold Palmer	5 ft 10 in
Nick Faldo	6 ft 3 in	Tony Jacklin	5 ft 9 in
Tiger Woods	6 ft 1 in	Bernhard Langer	5 ft 9 in
Colin Montgomerie	6 ft 1 in	Tom Watson	5 ft 9 in
Byron Nelson	6 ft 1 in	Bobby Jones	5 ft 8 in
Greg Norman	6ft 0 in	Gary Player	5 ft 7 in
Seve Ballesteros	6ft 0 in	Lee Trevino	5 ft 7 in
Sandy Lyle	6 ft 0 in	Ben Hogan	5 ft 7 in
Sam Snead	5 ft 11 in	Gene Sarazen	5 ft 5.5 in
Billy Casper	5 ft 11 in	Ian Woosnam	5 ft 4.5 in

The greatest golfer of all time!

Many have asked who is the greatest golfer who ever lived and one name naturally springs immediately to mind: Kim Jong Il, Dear Leader of the Democratic People's Republic of Korea (i.e. North Korea), Chairman of the National Defense Commission, Supreme Commander of the Korean People's Army and General Secretary of the Workers' Party of Korea.

And of course as should also be added to his list of titles, Greatest Golfer The World Has Ever Seen!

OK, he may not have won that many international golfing championships but his ability is clearly extraordinary. The North Korean Ministry of Information reported in November 1994 that Kim Jong Il had hit five holes-in-one during a single game!

Not only that but the Dear Leader had completed all 18 holes at the 7,700-yard championship course at Pyongyang in just 34 shots. It was the best round in history by some 25 shots. Suspicion was aroused however when it emerged that this had been Kim Jong-Il's first ever game of golf in his life. Not only that but he had never had a lesson!

But clearly the North Korean Ministry of Information would not lie about such an important matter.

No. It must have just been the greatest example of beginner's luck in history!

ACES AND OTHER EXTRAORDINARY SHOTS

A small hole-in-one!

Everyone's got to start somewhere, and what better way to start than with a hole-in-one?

Some people play golf their entire adult life without achieving this holey (sorry) grail. Then along comes some young whippersnapper and knocks one in without a by-your-leave. It shouldn't be allowed but all's fair in love and golf as Shakespeare never said.

The youngest player to achieve a hole-in-one was said to be Coby Orr. Five year old Coby of Littleton, Colorado hit his hole-in-one at the 103 yard 5th at the Riverside Club in San Antonio, Texas in 1975.

Twelve years later however Coby discovered he had a challenger. Matthew Draper got his at the ripe old age of 5 years and 212 days old at the Cherwell Edge Golf club in Oxfordshire on June 17, 1997. Impressively, it was on the 122-yard 4th hole.

Frustratingly for both Matthew and Coby, Christian Carpenter then scored a hole-in-one at the 5th hole of the Henry River Golf Course, Hickory, North California on 18th December 1999. Christian was just 4 years and 195 days old at the time. A stone plaque next to the 5th now commemorates the event.

And if that isn't ridiculous enough, in 2001 Jake Paine was playing at the Lake Forest (California) Golf and Practice Center when he teed off from the sixth and holed out. Although this was a mini-ace from 65 yards, it was still an impressive feat as Jake was aged just 3!

For his part Tiger Woods was a veritable veteran of six years old before he shot his first hole-in-one.

A hole-in-one is amazing when you think of the different universes this white mass of molecules has to pass through on its way to the hole.

Mac O'Grady

Old holes-in-one

But although not all players are so fortunate in the early days of their game, they should never give up because the golfing genie can wave his magic wand at any time.

The oldest person ever to get a hole-in-one was Elsie McLean who achieved hers at the age of 102 at the Bidwell Park course in Chico, California in 2007. The 100-yarder was the very first hole-in-one of her life.

In January 1985, 99 year old Otto Bucher from Switzerland became the oldest person to make a hole-in-one at the 130 yard 12th hole of La Manga Golf Course in Spain.

Harold Stilson, from Boca Raton, Florida was 101 years old when he went onto break the record when he hit an ace at the 108 yard 16th hole of the Deerfield Country Club on May 16, 2001.

At the Open Championship at Troon in 1973, Gene Sarazen hit a hole-in-one at the 8th hole (the 'Postage Stamp'). Sarazen was 71 years old at the time. He had first played at Troon at the 1923 Open, 50 years earlier!

Extraordinary holes-in-one

The first recorded hole-in-one at the British Open Championship was in 1868 at Prestwick when Young Tom Morris holed his tee shot at the 145 yard 8th hole.

In 1961 Lou Kretlow set a world record when he scored a hole-in-one on the 427 yard par 4 16th hole at Lake Hefner Golf Club, Oklahoma City. Kretlow wasn't even a professional golfer. He was a baseball player!

In 1971 at the Royal Norwich golf club, 25 year old John Hudson hit a hole-in-one at the 11th and then immediately followed it up with a second ace at the 12th. The 11th hole was 195 yards par 3 while the 12th was 311 yards par 4. This is believed to be the only time a player has scored two holes-in-one at consecutive holes in a major professional tournament.

One of the most amazing feats in the history of golf occurred early in the second round of the 1989 US Open held at Oak Hill Country Club, Rochester, New York. In just two hours four players all scored holes in one at the same hole. In turn Doug Weaver, Mark Wiebe, Jerry Pate and Nick Price aced the 167 yard sixth hole. Later that day, after he made a birdie-2, Fred Funk told the crowd, 'I can't believe you're clapping for a birdie!'

In 1983 Scott Palmer hit 28 holes-in-one all on par 3 and par 4 holes between 130 yards and 350 yards in length. In the 12 months from June 1983 to June 1984, he hit 33 holes-in-one. Overall he recorded over 100 aces.

What are the chances?

According to one expert the odds for making a hole-in-one on a par 3 hole are roughly 12,500 to 1 for an amateur golfer and 2,500 to 1 for a professional. The odds of two players both make a hole-in-one on the same hole during a single event are 32,000 to 1. The odds of making two holes in one during a single round of golf have been calculated as 67 million to one and three holes in one on consecutive par 3 holes are 156,250,000 to 1.

Taking a short cut

Most holes-in-one occur on par 3 holes. There have however been a number of holes-in-one scored on par 4 and even par 5 holes. In 1995, Shaun Lynch aimed straight toward the green on the horse-shoe shaped par 5 17th hole of Teign Valley Golf Club in Christow, England. He managed to clear a 20 foot hedge beyond which a down slope carried his ball to the green and straight into the hole.

In 1962 Larry Bruce had achieved a similar hole-in-one driving his ball over the top of a range of pine trees on the par 5 480 yard 5th hole at Hope Country Club, Arkansas.

Or, doing it the hard way instead, in 2002 Mike Crean made an ace on the straight par 5 9th hole at Green Valley Ranch Golf Club, Denver. His shot was 517 yards in length.

Holes-in-one insurance

Next time you hold a golf tournament, you might like to add a little zest to the proceedings by offering a special prize to the first lucky b... er, fortunate person who gets a hole-in-one. If you're offering perhaps a car, or a luxury holiday for two at Palm Springs it may be wise to take some insurance out because if you don't, as sure as eggs is eggs, someone's probably going to fluke a hole-in-one.

Luckily, there are now several insurance companies out there who will offer such insurance. As it has been estimated that the odds of an average golfer getting a hole-in-one are around 12,500 to 1 that means that you will make the ultimate shot once in every 666 (that sounds ominous doesn't it?) games. If you play once a week, expect your first hole in one after about 12 years and eight months. But if you play every day, you should have one after just 20 months. Don't hold your breath though...

In the lap of the golfing gods

In 2005, Tiger Woods played one of his most amazing shots. It was in the Masters, at the 16th hole.

The ball is right on the edge of the green, 30 feet from the hole, along a very complicated line; Tiger has to play uphill, and the rough is immediately behind the ball. No sweat. He chips the ball up past the hole, and it rolls back in a graceful curve, right back to the lip of the cup. Everyone (maybe even Tiger, too) thinks that that is where it will stay, and so it does for perhaps a second, then plop! It's in, the crowd goes wild, the commentators reach for their thesauruses of superlatives and Tiger adds another bit of stardust to his legend.

The fundamental problem with golf is that every so often, no matter how lacking you may be in the essential virtues required of a steady player, the odds are that one day you will hit the ball straight, hard, and out of sight. This is the essential frustration of this excruciating sport. For when you've done it once, you make the fundamental error of asking yourself why you can't do this all the time. The answer to this question is simple: the first time was a fluke.

Colin Bowles

Putt luck

Now, is any golfer going to admit that luck ever played a part in their best shots? Probably not, so let's just say that these are some of the most amazing shots ever seen in golf...

Did the earth move for you?

At the 2006 Allianz Championship Fuzzy Zoeller teed off from the 16th and played a not bad shot with the ball ending up just on the edge of the green in the rough. But then something strange happened. After a pause of maybe two or three seconds the ball started to move again! The golf genie had obviously sprinkled a bit of fairy dust on Zoeller's ball and it began to move towards the hole. And it kept on moving, slowly, but surely, until it plopped into the hole and amazed everyone watching. Extraordinary stuff!

Divine retribution

One Sunday morning the Reverend Simms asks his fellow vicar to take the morning service as he is feeling unwell. The Reverend Simms then takes the opportunity to sneak off to the local course for a crafty round of golf. From up above God and Saint Peter are keeping an eye on what the vicar is up to. 'I trust that you're going to punish that man,' says Saint Peter. 'Of course,' says God. 'Watch this!' And when the vicar tees off, the ball ricochets off three trees, flits across a pond, bounces off a rock, lands on the green and drops neatly into the hole. 'But,' says Saint Peter, 'I thought you said you were going to punish him?' 'I just have,' says God. 'Think about it! Who's he going to be able to tell?'

In off the white

In 2009 at the Canadian Open Leif Olsen played an amazing hole-in-one at the 15th. The ball hit the green above the hole, and in what can only be described in snooker terms, screwed back, cannoned off his opponent's ball and went in! Not only did Olsen have the satisfaction of playing the most amazing shot of the tournament he also won a BMW Z4 Roadster worth $50,000. Not bad eh?

Going for a long drive

At the US National Seniors Open Championship at Las Vegas on 25th September 1974, Mike Austin drove his ball an astonishing 515 yards. Austin was playing the par 4 450 yard 5th hole of Winterwood Course. A 35 mph wind helped his ball roll 65 yards past the flag. The ball was found on the next tee by Chandler Harper, Austin's companion that day. Austin was 64 years old at the time the record was set.

In September 1984 at Baldonnel Military Airport, Dublin Liam Higgins drove a ball 634.1 yards. In September 1990 Kelly Murray drove a ball 684.8 yards on the runway at Fairmont Hot Springs, British Columbia.

The little green man on the green

One day on a course in Ireland a golfer is struggling during a tournament. Suddenly, a leprechaun pops out of the third hole and offers to help him man out. 'I'll give you a hand every time you get in trouble,' says the little green man. 'What's the catch?' asks the golfer. 'I'll help you out,' explains the leprechaun, 'but every time I do, it will cost you one year of your sex life.' The golfer agrees and over the next few holes the leprechaun has to help him out of trouble ten times. At the end of the tournament the man is proclaimed the winner. After he has picked up his trophy, the leprechaun accosts him in the car park. Chuckling and rubbing his hands with glee, the leprechaun tells him, 'Well, you great eejit! That's going to cost you ten years off your sex life. And all just to win a little golf trophy. I hope you think it was worth it.' 'Well, yes,' says the man. 'I think it was.' 'Then more fool you!' laughs the leprechaun, pulling out his notebook. 'Now what's your name?' 'Father Murphy,' replies the man.

IT SHOULDN'T HAPPEN
TO A GOLFING VET

The next time things aren't going too well for you on the golf course take heart! It happens to the best of 'em. And don't forget, when things aren't going your way at least there aren't thousands of pounds at stake. At least, we hope not, unless you're richer than you've been letting on.

Greg Norman at The 1996 Masters

In the 1996 Masters Greg Norman went into the last round with a six shot lead over Nick Faldo. It was looking good. Maybe too good? Greg had set a course record of just 63 in the first round – how could he possibly fail?

Bogeys and double bogeys followed, then horror of horrors, a shot into the water on the twelfth. By the time he reached the end Greg had clocked up 78, and Faldo, with 67, had a major

title and walked away with $180,000 more than Norman's $270,000 runner-up prize.

After the match Norman said, 'All this was just a test. I just don't know what the test is yet.'

Golfer: I know you may find it hard to believe but I've never played this badly before.

Caddie: I find it hard to believe that you've played before at all.

Sam Snead and the US Open

You and golfing great Sam Snead have got something in common – neither of you has won the US Open. In fact Snead shares the dubious honour being one of the few players to come second on four occasions (the others were Arnold Palmer, Bobby Jones and Jack Nicklaus, so he was in good company). And if you think that's tough spare a thought for Phil Mickelson – he's been runner-up no fewer than five times!

Sam Snead not only came second on four occasions, he came so close to winning a couple of times that it was painful. In the 1939 US Open he only needed a par five on the final hole but ended up with eight. In the 1947 final he missed a 30-inch putt on the final hole and lost to Lew Worsham.

Two golfers are sitting at the 19th hole discussing their games. One tells the other, 'Do you know, my game has been so bad this year I've had to have my ball retriever re-gripped!'

The record you
really wouldn't want

The worst performance at a single hole in a competitive
event is said to have occurred in the qualifying round of the
Shawnee Invitational For Ladies held at Shawnee-on-Delaware,
Pennsylvania in 1912.

One player whose name has been lost to history teed off at
the 16th hole only to land her ball in the nearby Binniekill River
where it sat floating. The lady golfer then boarded a rowing boat
with her husband at the oars and set out in pursuit of the ball.
Her husband studiously kept count of every attempt she made to
swipe at the ball as it bobbed along the river. Eventually the ball
was beached one and a half miles downstream. She then had to
play through a forest on her way back. Her fellow competitors
had given up hope of seeing the lady again and were surprised
to hear her cry of 'fore' as she re-appeared from a completely
unexpected direction to complete the hole almost two hours after
teeing off.

Her final score for the 130 yard par 4 hole: 166 strokes.

Golf can best be defined as an endless series of tragedies obscured
by the occasional miracle followed, and by a good bottle of beer.

Anon

The world's worst golfing partner

George's wife asks him why he's stopped playing with his regular
golfing partner, Hugo. 'Answer me this,' replies George, 'would
you want to carry on playing with a man who was always
getting drunk. Would you want to carry on playing with a man

who was always losing his golf balls so other groups had to always play through? Would you want to carry on playing with a man who tells awful jokes all the time you're trying to putt and who repeatedly offends everyone he meets at the golf club?' 'Well in that case,' says the wife, 'no, I certainly wouldn't want to play with a man like that.' 'No,' says George sadly. 'And neither did Hugo.'

I can't believe things are going so well!

Ever had that situation when things are going really well, then as soon as somebody says how well they're going they stop going quite so well?

In 1961 Arnold Palmer was playing at the Masters and just needed to par on the 18th hole to be the first player to win the tournament two years running.

As he was teeing up someone in the crowd congratulated him on 'doing it again.' Arnie graciously thanked him, but alas, his concentration had been broken and he ended up going into a bunker and double-bogeying to let Gary Player in to win by a single shot.

Watch the birdie

Another legendary upset in a classic golf tournament and still talked about in hushed tones by golfers everywhere is Sam Snead's finish at the 1939 US Open.

Sam reached the 18th only needing a par five to win, but had somehow got it his head that he needed to birdie. So, instead of taking it easy he went for a big shot and went into the rough. He ended up triple-bogeying and tied for fifth place. There, does any of that make you feel better about when your games didn't go right? No? Thought not.

Arnie will be back!

In the 1960 US Open, Arnold Palmer began the final round seven shots behind and went on to win. History repeated itself in 1966... but not in a good way! That year Palmer had a seven-shot lead going into the final round but lost the lot over the course of the remaining 9 holes!

Golfer: Do you know what? I think you must be the worst caddie in history.
Caddie: No, I don't think so. That would be too much of a coincidence.

Highest score at the Open

The highest score for a single hole in the British Open Championship is believed to be 21 scored by a player in the first tournament at Prestwick in 1860.

Bear in mind though that overall scores in the 100s were not unusual in the early days of the Open and in 1883 at Musselburgh, Willie Fernie scored a 10 on one hole but nevertheless went on to win the competition. It is (so far!) the only time a champion has had a double-digit score for a single hole in the Open's history.

What a whiff!

In the 1983 British Open, Hale Irwin had been on the leader board until the 14th hole. He missed a 20-foot birdie putt and so had to tap the ball in from about two inches away. Guess what! He whiffed it!

Irwin later commented, 'It was just carelessness. The putter I used then – and I've just brought it back – had a flat back, like a Bullseye. I had a four inch putt and I just stuck it in the ground left-handed. It was an unintended sword fight. It happened in the third round and to say I would have won is stretching it. I would've gotten into a playoff. I regret the carelessness.'

In the end Irwin finished one shot behind the winner, Tom Watson.

They called it golf because all of the other four-letter words were taken.

Raymond Floyd

Have you ever noticed what golf spells backwards?

Al Boliska

It would make a grown man weep

Any golf tournament nicknamed the 'War on the Shore' ain't going to be a walk in the park. This was the 1991 Ryder Cup being played at Kiawah Island, South Carolina.

Mark Calcavecchia, who had won the British Open in 1989, was playing against Colin Montgomorie. Monty was making his debut for the European team.

Calcavecchia took a 5 up lead over the first nine holes. By the time he reached the final four holes Calcavecchia was still 4 ahead. A win on any of the remaining holes would mean he would win the cup for the US team.

He went on to fail to win all four holes. Plus for good measure at the 17th he hit a ball into the water, earning himself a half instead of the full point he should have taken.

Calcavecchia thought he had just single-handedly lost the Ryder Cup for the USA. He walked down onto the beach from the 18th green, sank down on the sand and cried. Amazingly however the US did go on to win the cup.

On the last day the scores for the Europe team and the US team were tied at eight apiece. Everything was hanging on the last hole of the last match between Europe's Bernhard Langer and the USA's Hale Irwin. Langer only needed to pull off a six-foot putt to secure a tie for Europe. Only! Now if you think you're under pressure with a couple of mates watching you trying to play a winning stroke, imagine how much pressure Langer was under. Don't forget, the Americans were hungry for this win. They hadn't taken the Ryder Cup home since 1983. Whether it was simply the huge pressure or something else we shall never know, but Langer missed a 6-foot par putt on the final hole.

The USA won by 14 ½ to 13 ½ points.

So in the end Calcavecchia's half point came in quite handy after all.

Putts get real difficult the day they hand out the money.

Lee Trevino

During a tournament at Peacehaven, Sussex in 1890, a Mr A J Lewis took an incredible 156 putts on a single hole! And he still failed to sink the ball!

It took me 17 years to get 3,000 hits in baseball. I did it in one afternoon on the golf course.

Babe Ruth

A terrible loss

Late one night Rory gets a call from his golf-mad friend, Winston. Winston is clearly in a desperate state. 'I can't believe it,' he sobs down the phone. 'I've just found out my wife's been having an affair for the past year with my golfing partner. Now they've run off together.' 'Come on, Winston old man!' says Rory. 'Pull yourself together. There are plenty of other women out there, you know.' 'I know that,' says Winston. 'It's him I'm worried about. He was the only golfer I know that I'm capable of beating!'

At least I shouted something

Dudley hits a wicked slice off the tee that ricochets through the trees and into the next fairway, narrowly missing another golfer. When Dudley finds his ball he also finds the other golfer who is in a very irate state following the near miss. 'I'm sorry,' says Dudley. 'I didn't have time to yell fore.' 'That's funny,' says the other golfer, 'because I noticed you had plenty of time to yell s***!'

If profanity had an influence on the flight of the ball, the game of golf would be played far better than it is.

Horace G. Hutchinson

The interesting thing about a golfer's language is that to listen to him one would think that his bad shots came as a surprise.

If you wish to hide your character, do not play golf.

Percey Boomer

Men who would face torture without a word become blasphemous at the short 14th. It is clear that the game of golf may well be included in that category of intolerable provocations which may legally excuse or mitigate behaviour not otherwise excusable.

A.P. Herbert

Q: What's the difference between a golfer and a skydiver?
A: One goes WHACK 'damn!' the other goes 'damn!' WHACK.

For Hoch's sake!

In 1989 Scott Hoch almost won a major championship. He could have claimed a place in golfing history by winning the 1989 Masters at Augusta National Golf Club. Unfortunately he claimed a place in golfing history for himself for the wrong reasons.

After the 16th hole, Hoch needed just two pars to win the Masters. But by the 18th Hoch and Nick Faldo had ended up tied. The game therefore went to a sudden death play off. On the first hole of the play off, Faldo struggled to a bogey 5. Hoch had another chance to win the Masters if he could two putt. He three putted.

His birdie putt rolled about 2 ½ feet past the hole. Hoch then spent two minutes examining the shot from every angle. He stepped up to take the shot then backed off again and thought about it a bit more. Eventually he took the shot. The ball didn't even touch the hole as it rolled five feet past it. On the next hole Faldo sank a 25 footer and won the Masters.

The phrase 'Hoch as in choke' subsequently entered golf terminology. Never mind though! Overall in his career Hoch won 11 times on the PGA Tour, played on two US Ryder Cup teams, earned almost $20 million and presumably spent considerable time trying hard not to think about that putt in the 1989 Masters.

Taking the Mickelson

Phil 'Lefty' Mickelson could easily have become US Open champion in 2006. He didn't.

Mickelson had not won any of the first 46 major championships in which he had competed. After this he brilliantly managed to change his approach and his fortunes. He reined back his aggression and improved his course decision making. He went on to win the 2004 Masters, the 2005 PGA Championship and the 2006 Masters.

And then came the 2006 US Open. Unexpectedly, Mickelson reverted to the form of his early career. On the 17th hole he managed to hit a rubbish bin but by the 18th he still had a one stroke lead. Despite having only managed to hit two fairways during the day, he decided to hit a driver on the final hole of the tournament. Sure enough he missed the fairway again although he did manage to hit the roof of a corporate hospitality tent.

The ball bounced off and landed in some rough grass. Mickelson could have safely got the ball back onto the fairway and gone on to par the hard way or bogey to get into the play off. But why play it safe? Instead he gave the ball a mighty slice. It flew up. It soared in the air. It hit a tree branch. It landed 25 yards from his feet.

This strategy having obviously failed, Mickelson immediately tried it once again. He gave the ball another hefty slice. And luckily this time it didn't hit a tree branch. It landed in a bank bunker instead. Mickelson double bogeyed and ended one shot out of a play off.

After the event Mickelson mused philosophically on the proceedings: 'I still am in shock that I did that. I just can't believe that I did that. I am such an idiot.'

On the plus side Mickelson holds the record for coming second in the US Open most often having achieved this on five occasions.

They throw their clubs backwards, and that's wrong. You should always throw a club ahead of you so that you don't have to walk any extra distance to get it.

Tommy Bolt

Real golfers, no matter what the provocation, never strike a caddie with the driver. The sand wedge is far more effective.

Huxtable Pippey

His master's voice

Rory and Winston are out playing golf and Rory has brought his small Yorkshire Terrier with him. Winston is impressed to see that whenever Rory hits a good shot the little dog stands up on his hind legs and gives his master a round of applause. 'That's most impressive,' says Winston. 'But what does the little fellow do when you hit a bad shot?' 'Well,' says Rory, 'usually he turns three somersaults. But to be honest it all depends on how hard I kick him.'

———

Golfer: Funny old game golf isn't it?
Caddie: Yes. But it's not meant to be.

The perfect shot

Archie is at the 18th hole of his local course preparing to tee off. He spends what seems like an eternity looking up, looking down, measuring the distance and working out the direction and speed of the wind. After several minutes of this his golfing partner can't stand it any more. 'For goodness sake, Archie,' says his partner, 'will you just get a move on and hit the blasted ball!' 'I can't,' says Archie nodding at the club house, 'my wife is over there watching us so I have to make sure I make the perfect shot.' 'Well you can forget that,' says his friend. 'You've got no hope of hitting her from here!'

Butterfingers!

In 2001 Scottish golfer Raymond Russell was well on his way to the final round of the English Open Championship which were being held that year at the Marriott Forest of Arden. He was just two holes away from a top 10 finish when disaster struck. Or should that be sploshed?

Russell was on the 17th green when he threw his ball to his caddie for a quick clean and polish prior to putting. The caddie fumbled at the ball for a moment before it rolled away behind him and plopped into an adjacent lake.

The ball could not be retrieved. Russell was given a two-stroke penalty and lost over £4,000 in prize money.

You have to wonder. If they ever drain that lake, might they find a caddie at the bottom complete with a strategically placed golf ball?

Golfer: I'm a terrible golfer. There can't be any golfers worse than me.
Caddie: There are plenty. They just don't play any more.

GOLF GEAR
Clothes by golf

If anything has contributed to the uncool image of golf over the years it has to be the clothes. Lairy Rupert the Bear checked trousers, comfy pastel shade sweaters, Argyle socks, spats, plus fours... Golf, it seems has a long history of sartorial faux pas stacked up against it.

But all that has changed. Apart from a new breed of younger players who have rebelled against the Pringlocracy of previous generations we now have some of the world's top designer names bringing out ranges of golfing wear. Armani, Hugo Boss, Ralph Lauren, Escada have all bought out their own collections of golf clothes.

The name though that is most readily associated with golf wear though is that of Pringle. Who are they? Well naturally, they're a Scottish company. They began in the Borders in 1815 and they claim to have invented not only the Argyle or Intarsia design (the diamond pattern that crops up on golfing cardies) but also the twin set as well. So, they have quite a lot to answer in for in some people's minds, though others swear by the brand.

So is Pringle back in vogue? Is it cool or uncool? They have no shortage of celebrity wearers from Madonna to David Beckham, but then Pringle was also a favourite of Alan Partridge, so that doesn't help, but in the end does it matter? Pringle have been around for almost 200 years and may well be around for another 200 and golfers all over the world are still wearing their clothes.

Red coats

Golfers playing over public ground used to wear red coats. This was to make them visible to other passers by and so warn people they might be struck down by a flying golf ball at any moment!

What's that in your golf trousers?

One Saturday morning Angus's car breaks down and he is forced to catch the bus to get to the golf course. He fills his golf bag so full that the only way he can carry an extra spare pair of balls is to stuff them into his trouser pockets. Angus catches the bus, heaves his bag into the luggage rack and plonks himself down opposite an old lady. After a few moments Angus becomes aware of the old lady staring at the strange bulge that he has in his bright tartan golfing trousers. Angus leans over to the old lady and whispers to her, 'Don't worry, madam. It's just my golf balls.' 'Oh dear,' says the old lady. 'So is that similar to tennis elbow?'

Expensive feathery balls

Everyone knows what a golf ball looks like right? It's small, it's white and it has dimples – the sporting equivalent of Shirley Temple. But it wasn't always this way. When golf kicked off in the fifteenth century they were using wooden balls. The clubs were wooden too.

Then in the early 1600s the 'featherie' was introduced. This was made by putting goose feathers (enough to fill a top hat!) into a bull's hide exterior. The bull's hide was first hand-stitched inside-out leaving a quarter of an inch slit. The next job was to turn the ball outside in and was extremely difficult. Following this the top hat's-worth of feathers had to be stuffed into the ball using a long spike. The quarter-inch slit was then sewn up and the whole thing soaked in water to make the leather shrink and the feathers expand. This produced a nice solid ball which was waterproofed with white lead paint.

A good golf ball maker might make three such balls in a day. Because of the labour-intensive manufacture these balls were extremely expensive to buy. In fact the featheries required so much skill to produce that they cost three times as much as a golf club.

And after all that, the balls didn't last long and would become soggy if they got wet.

As if that could ever happen on a golf course!

New balls please

Dylan is waiting for Harris to tee off ahead of him. Harris however is taking ages. He keeps producing a brand new ball from his bag and unwrapping it before slicing it away into the trees. Each time the ball disappears Harris mutters a curse and reaches into his bag for yet another brand new ball which he again promptly loses. 'Erm, excuse me, old man,' interrupts Dylan, 'why don't you try using an old ball instead?' Harris looks over at him and says through gritted teeth, 'Because I've never bloody had an old one!'

Guttie gracious me

The featherie was around for over 200 years until the 'Guttie' was introduced in 1848 by the Reverend Adam Paterson of (where else?) St Andrews, Scotland. 'Guttie' was short for Gutta-Percha, the tree from whose sap the ball was made. The Guttie

was cheaper than the featherie and it was discovered that if there were imperfections in the surface of the ball it flew straighter. The manufacturers then started to put deliberate indentations onto the surface of the ball which became the dimple that we know and love today.

Idling with a length of rubber

The Guttie ruled until 1898 when one Coburn Haskell of Cleveland, Ohio invented the modern ball. Haskell developed the idea for the modern golf ball in an idle moment in the same way that small boys make balls by wrapping rubber bands around each other.

Haskell was himself an avid golfer and one day in 1898 he had a game of golf arranged with his friend, Bertram Work. Work was superintendent of the B.F. Goodrich rubber factory in Akron, Ohio.

While Haskell waited for his golfing partner he began winding a long rubber thread and forming it into a ball. Haskell discovered that when he bounced the finished ball, it flew almost to the ceiling. Bertram Work suggested covering the rubber with gutta percha and together the pair began manufacturing the first modern golf balls.

To begin with however, the winding of the rubber was done by hand and was not particularly successful. Mechanization of the

process enabled the elastic to be stretched tighter and as a result performance improved significantly. Eventually balata was used to coat the balls rather than gutta-percha.

The new ball was as durable as the gutty but it was softer and thus did not damage the face of a golf club so badly. And it's always handy to have a ball that won't wreck your clubs.

There was also another design around in the late 1800s, the Bramble, which had raised bumps instead of dimples.

If you think it's hard to meet new people, try picking up the wrong golf ball.

Jack Lemmon

A round with the mother-in-law

One Sunday Angus is having a round of golf with his mother-in-law. At the third hole she slices the ball into a field next to the golf course. Angus and his mother in law climb over the fence and start looking for her ball. They search all over but can't find the ball anywhere. Eventually Angus notices a cow in the corner of the field and realizes that the one place they haven't looked is next to the cow. He goes over, pokes around and then notices something sticking in the cow's backside. He lifts up the cow's tail and finds a golf ball securely lodged in the animal's nether regions. 'Hey!' he shouts over to his mother-in-law while pointing cheerfully at the cow's backside, 'does this one look like yours?!'

The man with
funny coloured balls

The first PGA pro to win a tournament using a coloured ball was Wayne Levi at the Hawaiian Open in 1982. The ball was orange!

Did you hear about the idiot golfer who invented green golf balls, so he could find them more easily in the sand traps?

What's for tee?

Dudley phones his doctor and says, 'Help! Doctor! It's an emergency! My two-year-old son has just swallowed my golf tees.' 'Don't worry,' says the doctor, 'I'll be there as soon as I can.' 'OK,' says Dudley, 'but is there anything I can be doing in the meantime?' 'Well,' says the doctor, 'I suppose you could practice your putting.'

All manner of balls

Today the collecting of antique golf balls is a popular pastime, and an expensive one. Some balls can fetch hundreds of pounds, though no one yet has found an example of one of the original wooden balls.

Golf balls were standardized in 1921 by the Royal and Ancient in the UK and the USGA (United States Golf Association) in the United States, so they had to have a fixed size and weight.

In the 1970s some bright spark invented a golf ball with a built-in radio transmitter which enabled players to find lost balls more easily. In more recent times someone else has come up with

a ball that can actually be controlled by radio! So, while your opponent isn't looking you pop one of these onto his tee and after he's hit it you can control where it goes. Great fun, just don't get caught! Especially if you're playing in the Ryder Cup at the time.

Note: Also, watch out for other novelty golf balls. These balls that do not conform to the usual standards and which have been developed for practical jokers include the exploding golf ball, the 'wobbler' which is weighted to go off the intended line of play, and the 'floater' which will not sink when knocked into a water hazard. There are others too which may not just be used by practical jokers, but by, not to put too fine a point on it, cheats.

The unloseable golf ball

Two friends, Joe and Bill, are playing golf one day when Bill suddenly notices Joe's ball.

'What's that ball you've got?' he asks. 'It's a strange colour.'

'It's luminous,' says Joe. 'If this baby goes into the woods I'll be able to see it glowing.'

'It won't help much if it goes into the water, will it?' says Bill.

'Ah, well that's where you're wrong,' says Joe. 'If it goes into the water it floats, and navigates itself to the nearest bank.'

'Clever!' says Bill. 'But what if goes in the long grass – how do you find it then?'

'It has a powerful light that flashes on and off and a bleeper sounds. I'm telling you this ball is completely unloseable.'

'Wow,' says Bill. 'So where did you get it?'

'Oh,' says Joe, 'I found it.'

Tee's up

Considering that golf had been around since at least the fifteenth century it took an awful long time for someone to invent the portable tee. It wasn't until 1899 that two Scotsmen (naturally) named William Bloxsom and Arthur Douglas came up with this invaluable aid to driving. Up till then golfers would make a 'tee' by piling up little mounds of sand. Originally the 'tee' just meant (as it still does today) the area from which golfers played their first shot to the hole. Bloxsom and Douglas's tee was a piece of rubber with prongs sticking up on which to rest the ball. It wasn't until the 1920s when American dentist Dr William Lovell came up with his 'Reddy Tee' that the mass marketing of something similar to today's tee began.

Buggy off

According to Mark Twain golf is a good walk spoiled, but does that still apply if you're riding in a golf buggy? Leaving aside the fact that one of the reasons some people are attracted to golf is the gentle exercise in walking from one hole to another, the golf buggy was probably a fabulous innovation when first introduced around 1951. The electric golf buggy was invented by American Merle Williams, who had developed his knowledge of electric engines during wartime fuel rationing.

But the golf buggy, or golf cart as the Americans prefer to call it, has found a life beyond the golf course. Some small communities such as those on the islands of Belize or in The Villages, a retirement community in Florida, use golf buggies instead of petrol-driven cars. In some other places motor vehicles are banned and golf buggies are used instead; for example, Hamilton island in Queensland, Australia. In the community of Discovery Bay in Hong Kong private vehicles are not allowed at all – apart from a fleet of over 500 golf buggies.

And if the phrase 'golf buggy' conjures up images of something rather feeble and slow, don't forget that up until the 1980s you could have bought a brand-new Harley–Davidson golf buggy! Perfect for those rock star golf aficionados!

Fans of cult TV may also remember that the golf buggy was the main form of transport in The Village in *The Prisoner* series. Except that it wasn't. Although the cars used as taxis in the Village sure look like golf buggies they were in fact Mini Mokes.

Going clubbing

It is believed that in the early days of what was to become golf players would use whatever wooden implement came to hand – e.g. a stick or a crook. As the game became more popular and formalized people would fashion their own 'clubs' from wood. The first known set of specially made clubs were those made for James IV of Scotland, who had commissioned a bow-maker to design them for him.

When James I became King of England in 1603 he appointed a royal club maker, one William Mayne, who made him another set of clubs. At this time a set of clubs would have included 'play' clubs for driving, 'fairway' clubs for medium length shots, 'spoons' for short shots, and niblicks to do the job of a modern eight or nine iron. The set would be completed with a 'cleek' for putting.

Even though it would have been possible to have made metal-headed clubs earlier in the history of golf wooden clubs stayed around for much longer because of the 'featherie' ball. As these were expensive and relatively delicate they would not have easily withstood the impact of a forged iron head.

In the late 1800s drop-forging had allowed the large-scale manufacture of irons, and by this time the 'featheric' ball had been superseded by the 'guttie', so the way was clear for this next development in golf club history.

Despite this however, wooden clubs were still being hand-made until the early years of the twentieth century. Steel shafts were tried out as early as the 1890s but not generally approved of to begin with. The Royal and Ancient only permitted their use after 1929 when the Prince of Wales wanted to use them on the old course at St Andrews. Well they could hardly say no could they?

At one time a golfer could take as many clubs on the course as he wanted to, but in 1939 the Royal and Ancient decreed that the maximum number of clubs allowed in a golfer's bag over a game was 14. In the same year they also introduced the numbering system for clubs. Although this may have been more efficient it was a shame to see those ancient (and largely Scottish) names disappear. The mashee, the niblick, the brassie, the spoon and the cleek were to be no more.

The first graphite clubs came into the game in the early 1970s, and since then there have been various refinements and improvements, partly due to computer-aided design as well as new manufacturing methods. But to quote an old song, whatever you do to improve the clubs it don't mean a thing if you ain't got that swing.

Golfers of course always carry a spare sock with them, just in case they get a hole-in-one...

A ROUND WITH ALICE

For many years golf had a rather cosy, middle-class, middle-aged, white, male image. The Conservative club at play, if you like. But then a certain rock star took the game up...

Alice Cooper

If you'd deliberately wanted to shake up the game what better person than a baby doll-decapitating, chicken-bothering, man in make-up with a woman's name? Actually, of course, that was just his stage act. In real life, he is Vincent Furnier, son of a preacher, and may well have had a secret habit of dressing up in Pringle sweaters even before he started playing golf.

In fact, Alice is said to play the game six days a week, has a handicap of just three and has since 1996 hosted the annual Alice Cooper Pro-Am Golf Tournament. This raises money for his Christian-based charity the Solid Rock Foundation. In 2007 he even called his autobiography *Alice Cooper, Golf Monster*.

Catherine Zeta-Jones

Again, as far from the middle-aged male as you can get, but in a rather different way. This Welsh/Hollywood glamourpuss played in the All*Star Cup in 2005, a celebrity golf tournament that Ant & Dec had come up with and which was held at the Celtic Manor resort in Newport.

Chris Evans

Another veteran of the All*Star Cup, Evans proved that it was possible to still be seen as a wild 'n' wacky DJ while wearing

retina-bothering trousers and wielding a putter. He even married a golf professional, Natasha Shishmanian in 2007, and in 2009 became a BBC commentator during the (British) Open Championship.

Swing it, Fred!

During a sequence in the 1938 film *Carefree*, Fred Astaire had to strike a dozen golf balls with a driver while dancing. Not only did he manage to accomplish this feat while keeping in rhythm, when the studio hands went to collect the golf balls afterwards, they were all said to be lying within eight feet of each other. Seeing as this technique clearly works, surely there should be more dancing golfers on the professional circuit!

Sylvester Stallone

If the Rocky star could swing a club as well as he could swing a punch, then yeah, maybe he coulda been a contender. As it happens, he has a respectable handicap of 11.4 according to *Golf Digest* magazine so maybe all that bicep-building came in handy after all.

Somebody once asked Muhammad Ali what he was like at golf. He replied, 'I'm the Greatest! I just haven't played yet!'

Humour writer Alan Coren was once told that the most popular subjects for books were cats, golf and Nazis. So he published a collection of essays called *Golfing For Cats*. The cover picture showed a cat in a Nazi uniform swinging a putter.

Class balls

The ordinary working man likes to spend his weekends talking about football. The lower middle classes like to spend their weekends talking about tennis. The upper middle classes like to spend their weekends talking about golf. So the conclusion is obvious: the higher up the social scale you are, the smaller your balls are.

More tee?

A golfer is giving a non-golfing friend a lift in his new Honda car when the friend notices a couple of golf tees left in the glove compartment. 'What the hell are these for?' asks the friend. 'They're tees,' explains the golfer, 'you use them to put your balls on when you're driving.' 'Wow!' says his friend looking at the rest of the car, 'those Japanese think of everything.'

Jack Nicholson

Hell-raising, womanizing, beyond middle-age party animal Nicholson would seem not to be your typical Pringle-clad practitioner of putts that would actually wait until the 19th hole before cracking open the Jack Daniels. But the man who made 'Wendy, I'm home' the most chilling back-from-the-office greeting ever has been playing for almost 20 years. Where did he find the time? He was also involved in a rare celebrity golf-related road-rage incident. Stuck in traffic in 1994 he is said to have jumped out of his car and smashed another driver's windscreen. What club does one use for such an occasion? Jack used a 2-iron.

What's in the Name?

Golfing great Arnold Palmer once played a friendly game of golf with Frank Sinatra. 'So,' said Frank after the round, 'how do you like my game?' 'Well,' said Arnie, 'I prefer golf!'

Clint Eastwood

Well, are you feeling lucky punk? Not if the 18 holes are bullet wounds from Dirty Harry. But of course there is a lighter side to Clint Eastwood away from the tough-guy roles he's known for. He is a keen golfer and even owns his own club, the Tehama Golf Club at Carmel, California.

Dennis Hopper

From *Easy Rider* to Ryder Cup? Surely not. Well not quite, but the anti-star of such unpleasant roles as Frank Booth in David Lynch's *Blue Velvet*, as well as the aforementioned motorcycle-riding star of hippie spaced odyssey *Easy Rider*, does enjoy a potter with a putter. In fact, come to think of it, Jack Nicholson was in *Easy Rider* too. Surely their shared interest in golf doesn't go back *that* far? Dennis Hopper has been quoted as saying, 'The greatest thrill in the world is hitting a good golf shot.'

This from a man who at one time was alleged to have been rather keen on drink and drugs. He is said to have played golf with country singer Willie Nelson between takes for his role in *Texas Chainsaw Massacre II*.

When the entertainer Sammy Davis Junior was asked about his golf handicap he said, 'My handicap? Man, I am a one-eyed, black Jew! *That's* my handicap!'

Groucho Marx was once asked by a reporter whether he wanted to play Hamlet. 'No,' said Groucho. 'Not unless he gives me a stroke a hole!'

Sharon Stone

Playing golf may not be many men's first thought when the name Sharon Stone comes up, but the *Basic Instinct* star has been playing the game since high school. Though she is said to have played on the boys' team! There was no girls' team and she insisted on playing. In response her teacher is said to have made her get changed in the boys' changing rooms. With her *Basic Instinct* co-star Michael Douglas also being a keen player perhaps that film could have just as easily have been about golf. Or maybe not...

Meat Loaf

The larger-than-life sweat-stained rock 'n' rolling Mr Loaf is not perhaps the first person you'd think of as being up for the fresh air and exercise that a round of golf entails, but he was one of the US celebrity team in the 2006 All*Star Cup. He played alongside other unlikely golfers such as the above-mentioned Alice Cooper, as well as actress Jane Seymour, who despite being British, was playing for the American team.

Cheryl Ladd

Though better known for chasing criminals as one of *Charlie's Angels*, Cheryl Ladd likes nothing better than to chase that elusive scratch handicap on the golf course. In 2005 she even wrote a book about golf entitled *Token Chick: A Woman's Guide to Golfing With The Boys*. And the boys had better watch out – she has a handicap of just 14.

While out golfing one day, President George W. Bush was asked to comment on a suicide bombing in Israel the previous day. He said, 'I call upon nations to do everything they can to stop these terrorist killers.' He then to the assembled reporters and said: 'Thank you. Now, watch this drive.'

Arnold Schwarzenegger

Just what you need when you stroll out onto the first fairway isn't it? To find that you're playing a cyborg who can not only rebuild his own body organs but probably rebuild yours too if you dare to win. Though that of course was Arnie's old job, and today he is a politician. Mind you, would you dare to actually beat the Governor of California either?

The Pope and Cardinal Nicklaus

The Pope is meeting with the College of Cardinals to discuss a proposal from the President of Israel. 'Your holiness,' says one of the Cardinals, 'Mr Peres wishes to challenge you to a golf match that will determine whether Jews or Catholics are better.' The Pope is worried as he has never held a golf club in his life. 'Don't worry,' says the Cardinal, 'let's call Jack Nicklaus. We'll make him a Cardinal, he can play Shimon Peres... We can't lose!' Everyone agrees to the idea and the call is made to Jack Nicklaus who deems it an honour to play. The day after the match, Nicklaus reports to the Vatican and tells the Pope, 'I came second, your Holiness.' 'Second?!!' exclaims the surprised Pope. 'You came second to Shimon Peres?!!' 'No,' says Cardinal Nicklaus. 'I came second to Rabbi Woods.'

Stevie's handicap

Stevie Wonder and Tiger Woods are chatting together one night in a bar. Tiger is quite surprised to learn that Stevie is a keen golfer. 'I don't understand,' says Tiger. 'How can you play golf when you're blind?' Stevie replies, 'It works fine. I get my caddie to stand in the middle of the fairway and call to me. Then I just play the ball towards the sound of his voice.' Amazing,' says Tiger. 'So what's your handicap?' 'Actually I'm a scratch golfer,' says Stevie. 'Fantastic!' says Tiger. 'What do you say we play a round some time.' 'Definitely,' says Stevie. 'But I should warn you I usually play for $10,000 a hole.' 'Fine by me,' says Tiger shaking on the deal. 'So when are we going to play together?' 'It doesn't bother me,' says Stevie. 'Just pick any night you want!'

Stars of golf and screen

In 1931 Bobby Jones made a series of 12s golf instruction films under the title *How I Play Golf*. A couple of years later he made a further six films under the series title *How To Break 90*. Nothing unusual about a golfer making instructional films, but these ones starred a whole host of big Hollywood names including James Cagney, Loretta Young, Edward G. Robinson, Douglas Fairbanks Junior, and W.C. Fields. The films were directed by George Marshall, director of *How The West Was Won*.

Halle Berry

A golf-playing Bond girl? Whatever next? 007 has come a long way over the years in getting to grips with feminism, post-feminism, and the sort of women who have shaken him as well as stirred him, but luckily Halle Berry kept her golf-playing to her private life. The thought of Bond getting thrashed on the golf course would probably be too much for the legions of die-hard 007 fans to bear. In real life however, the Halle Berry Celebrity Golf Classic had its inaugural event in April 2008 in aid of the Jenesse Center charity.

Cameron Diaz

And why shouldn't golf have a bit of glamour? She'd probably even look good in checked trousers. She was introduced to the game in 2006 by her then-boyfriend Justin Timberlake, who is himself a keen golfer.

Bing Columbo

Bing Crosby was once offered the lead role in the TV detective series *Columbo* but he turned it down. He said the demands of the acting schedule would have interfered with his golf game.

Neil Young

Perhaps it's not surprising that Neil Young is a golfer. His mother was an amateur golf champion and his father was a sports writer. And Neil Young isn't one of the new breed of rock 'n' roll golfers who is following a trend. It is said that when he first went to LA in 1966 on joining Buffalo Springfield, one of the first things he asked was where the nearest golf course could be found.

After he had retired as US President, Dwight Eisenhower was asked whether leaving the White House had affected his golf game in any way. 'Yes,' he said, 'a lot more people beat me now!'

Patti Smith

Yes, punk poet, rock 'n' roller Patti Smith took up golf during her 15-year lay off from the music business in the years1980–95. She was taught the game by her new husband, Fred 'Sonic' Smith, a former member of the legendary hard rock band MC5, himself a rather unlikely exponent of the game.

It's all balls to me

Singer Christina Aguilera was once introduced to Tiger Woods who said, 'Oh, Christina, I love your music, I have all your CDs.' 'Sorry,' Aguilera replied. 'I don't follow tennis so I don't know much about you.'

Bob Dylan

Who would have thought that this icon of 60s counter-culture would end up becoming a golfer? But when *Golf Digest* magazine published its list of the top 100 musician golfers, who was at number 63 with a handicap of 17? Why none other than ol' gravel voice himself. Not only that, in 2004 Dylan accepted an honorary degree from St Andrews University (only the second one that he had ever accepted) and in 2007 he and his brother David bought the Aultmore House Estate in Scotland which just happened to be handy for the Abernethy golf club. Though the club treasurer, with the wonderfully aloof-sounding name of Jack McCool said that if he wanted to join 'Mr Dylan will have to apply in writing just like anyone else and be vetted by the committee.'

William Wordsworth

Romantic poet William Wordsworth famously described golf as a 'day spent in a round of strenuous idleness'. Except he didn't. The quote is from Book IV of Wordsworth's long autobiographical poem *The Prelude* but, despite its inclusion in many collections of golf-related quotations, the round referred to is not a round of golf! *The Prelude* is in fact a long meditation on the development of the poetic sensibility. It does not contain a single mention of the word 'golf' and is conspicuously lacking in any verses concerning Wordsworth's handicap!

Similarly Samuel Johnson once declared, 'It is unjust to claim the privileges of age, and retain the play-things of youth'. Again the good doctor did not have the pleasures of the fairway in mind at the time but nevertheless his words have since been adapted into the popular quotation: 'Golf: A game in which you claim the privileges of age and retain the playthings of youth.'

Golf-finger

In his 1959 novel *Goldfinger*, Ian Fleming gives a detailed account of a high-stakes game of golf between James Bond and arch villain Auric Goldfinger. Goldfinger attempts to cheat by switching balls but Bond eventually wins on a 'strict rules of golf' technicality.

The Royal St Mark's course described in the novel is closely modelled on the Royal St George's at Sandwich in Kent. The sixth hole at Royal St George's is called The Maiden. In Fleming's novel the 6th hole is The Virgin. There is a bunker on the 8th hole at Royal St George's called Hades. In the book the bunker at the eighth is Hell Bunker. The golf pro at Royal St George's was Alfred Whiting, the fictional pro at Royal St Mark's is Alfred Blacking. Surely even a secret agent of James Bond's calibre would have had trouble cracking a cipher of this level of complexity!

Ian Fleming lived at St Margaret's Bay not far from Sandwich and was himself a member of Royal St George's. Fleming was said to be a competent golfer who, like James Bond, had a handicap of nine.

It had in fact been during a game at Royal St George's that Fleming first heard the name Goldfinger. Fleming's golfing partner, businessman John Blackwell, told him that his cousin's husband was the architect Ernö Goldfinger. The name appealed to Fleming as suitably villainous and he thought he might use it in one of his books. A character called John Blackwell also makes an appearance in chapter one of the novel.

In the 1964 film starring Sean Connery, the golfing scenes were not filmed at Royal St George's. Instead Stoke Park Golf Course in Buckinghamshire was used as it was more convenient for Pinewood Studios. It was however during the filming of *Goldfinger* that Sean Connery first developed his love of the game.

A month before the film opened, Fleming was nominated to be club captain at Royal St George's. Sadly the nomination was passed the day before the author's death from a heart attack on August 12, 1964 at the age of 56.

P.G. Golf-house

P.G. Wodehouse, the creator of Jeeves and Bertie Wooster took up golf in 1920 and two years later produced a volume of ten short stories on the sport entitled *The Clicking of Cuthbert*.

Most of the stories are related by a character known as The Oldest Member, a retired golfer who sits in his chair at the nineteenth hole and regales his audiences of younger golfers with the sort of tales of victory and woe that all golfers will be familiar with – especially the woe. Maybe you've got a character like this at your club?

Over the years Wodehouse wrote many more golf stories – at least 30, and many of these have been collected and published in various anthologies. In 1926 he produced *The Heart of a Goof* containing nine more golfing stories. Then in 1950 came a collection of ten short stories entitled *Nothing Serious*, five of which were about golf.

Some of the titles give the flavour of Wodehouse's relationship with the game: *Ordeal By Golf, Those In Peril On The Tee*, and *The Long Hole*.

Although the stories were written a long time ago, some things in golf never change, and Wodehouse usually has a line that sums it up. For example, the way the slightest distraction can put you off your stroke. He wrote of someone missing short putts because of 'the uproar of butterflies in the adjoining meadows.'

When he wrote *Heart of a Goof*, Wodehouse pointed out that a lot of the people who reviewed his first book of golfing stories, *The Clicking of Cuthbert*, had stated in their defence that they were not golfers themselves. So he suggested that when people reviewed this volume they should be required to state their golfing handicap so readers would know how to seriously to take their comments!

Wodehouse also wrote that he wished he had taken up golf earlier (he was 39 when he did so, which he considered to be middle age) instead of 'footling about writing stories and things.' He believed that if had done so he might have got his handicap down below 18! Everyone assumes he was joking, but was he?

In the introduction to *The Clicking of Cuthbert* (published as *Golf Without Tears* in the USA) Wodehouse said that the book was 'written in blood.' Most golfers will probably know what he means by that, and he may have been deadly serious!

Rudyard Kipling

British author Rudyard Kipling is credited with the invention of snow golf. Following his marriage Kipling settled for a while in Vermont where he began writing *The Jungle Book* and the *Barrack Room Ballads*. Kipling was visited there by Sherlock Holmes author Sir Arthur Conan Doyle who, being a keen golfer, had brought his clubs with him. Following a lesson from Conan Doyle, Kipling took to golf and would even play in the snow using golf balls painted red. Kipling did not however think that 'snow golf' was 'altogether a success because there were no limits to a drive; the ball might skid two miles down the long slope to Connecticut river.' Others however might be of the opinion that Mr Kipling had invented an exceedingly good game of golf.

GOLF GOES TO HOLLYWOOD!

We're not talking about those golf instruction videos and DVDs cluttering your shelves, we're talking proper bona fide Hollywood films that are about your favourite sport. And there have been quite a few over the years, for example:

The Legend of Bagger Vance

This 2000 film was directed by Robert Redford no less, and starred Will Smith and Matt Damon. It brings in real-life golfers Walter Hagen (played by Bruce McGill) and Bobby Jones (played by Joel Gretsch). Most golfers will probably be able to relate to the story of a golfer battling personal demons, but perhaps not to playing with two of the legends of the game!

Tin Cup

Released in 1996, it stars Kevin Costner as a down-on-his-luck golf pro working at a driving range. He decides to try and impress a woman (played by Rene Russo) by winning the US Open (as you do). Does he do it? We wouldn't want to spoil it for you, but win or no win the woman's boyfriend, a professional golfer played by Don Johnson, is none too happy about her fraternising with Mr Driving Range.

Happy Gilmore

Also released in 1996 and starring Adam Sandler in the title role. Wannabe ice hockey player ends up playing golf and going on the PGA tour to raise money to regain granny's repossessed house. Look out for Ben Stiller in an uncredited role. Warning: may give nightmares to golfers everywhere due to alligator-in-water-hazard scene!

Caddieshack

1980 comedy film starring Bill Murray and Chevy Chase. Hard-up kid becomes caddie to help raise funds to get him through college. Golf course unfortunately has that all too familiar problem of a gopher chewing up the greens.

The Greatest Game Ever Played

2005 Disney film based on the true life story of American Francis Ouimet, who unexpectedly beat fancied Brits Harry Vardon and Ted Ray in the 1913 US Open. He was the first amateur ever to win the championship.

The Caddie

Dean Martin and Jerry Lewis film from 1953. Crazy comedy capers as the duo mess up as golfers and become entertainers instead – a sort of Dean Martin and Jerry Lewis in fact! The film is notable for including cameos by three of the world's best ever golfers, Ben Hogan, Byron Nelson and Sam Snead. It was also the first time anyone had ever heard the Dean Martin classic That's Amore which featured in the soundtrack.

Follow the Sun

This 1951 film is based on the life story of one of the all-time golfing greats, Ben Hogan, who is played by Glenn Ford. Look out for another golfing legend, Sam Snead, playing himself in the film.

Bobby Jones Stroke of Genius

Released in 2004 this follows the career of one of the best, and most interesting golfers ever. It stars Jim Caviezel in the title role. It is the only golfing film to have been granted permission to use the Royal and Ancient course at St Andrews for location filming. The film also stars Malcolm McDowell.

Dead Solid Perfect

A humorous 1988 film starring Randy Quaid as a struggling golf pro who is on the PGA tour. With his marriage in trouble too, the main character battles to keep everything together. Some have said that this is the best golf movie ever. The soundtrack is by Tangerine Dream.

Should Married Men Go Home?

All right, this is a short, rather than a full-length film, but it does star Laurel and Hardy in what was the first film of theirs to see them billed as a double act. Although it was released in 1928, it will probably still be of great comfort to golfers everywhere who know that however bad their game was today it will never be as bad as Stan and Ollie's!

GOLFMANSHIP

Golf was invented by some Scotsman who hit a ball, with a stick, into a hole in the ground. The game today is exactly the same, except that it now takes some 90-odd pages of small type to ensure that the ball is hit, with the stick, into the hole in the ground without cheating.

A.S. Graham

A beginner's introduction

To some, 'gamesmanship' means finding the edge, being smarter than your opponent, keeping one step ahead of him or her by whatever means possible. To others it means 'cheating'. You know the sort of thing we're talking about: people who sneeze loudly just as you're teeing off, people who make doubting comments about the club you've selected for a shot, people who phone your mobile just as you're trying to hit the ball out of the rough...

Then there are the more subtle tactics. Some players have been known to select the 'wrong' club from their bag just before their opponent plays so he perhaps thinks that 'hey, you know what' maybe I should be using a 1-iron on this 500-yard drive as well.' Then, after he has played a disastrous shot our gamesman pops his 1-iron back in his bag and selects his driver instead.

And it's not just aspiring amateurs who do this sort of thing. Gamesmanship has been seen at the highest levels of the game.

Professional gamesmanship

There have even been dark whispers about gamesmanship being deployed in events such as the Ryder Cup. Players jingling their small change in their pocket while the other player is in mid-backswing or perhaps coughing at a strategic moment. Others have been accused of walking off while their opponent is still putting on the green.

One famous incident, which some thought may have been gamesmanship, but others, including the 'victim' thought was just a bit of fun was at the 1971 US Open. Jack Nicklaus was playing Lee Trevino at the Merion golf club and just before they were about to tee off Lee Trevino reached into his golf bag and produced a snake! He wiggled the three-foot reptile around and threw it to Nicklaus just as he and the assembled press corps twigged that it was in fact a toy snake. Nicklaus took it all in good heart though you do wonder whether it may have slightly wrong-footed him. Trevino went on to win by three strokes.

'Putting' yourself first

Another trick that has been used is the 'putt concession'. Your opponent's ball is a couple of feet away from the hole, and you say, 'It's OK, I know you can hole that in your sleep so don't even waste time playing it.' You let a few of these go in the early stages of the game then, at the end when it's getting critical, and your opponent's nerves are perhaps slightly more frayed you don't give a concession. So he's suddenly on the spot, he's slightly rattled at your change of tune, plus, crucially, he's had no short putting practice the whole day! And the beauty of it is that you haven't broken a single rule. You can even believe that you've been playing the nice guy.

Other tactics include taking a long time to select your club for a shot; picking one out, putting it back, then selecting another one, putting that back and so on until your opponent's composure begins to wilt. Or, you can just play slowly, stand too close to your opponent when he's playing, or perhaps whistle, then stop, and just as he's about to play, apologize.

Beyond gamesmanship

Definite no-nos are:

- Actually taking a musical instrument with you to play between shots

- Sticking chewing gum to your opponent's ball to alter its flight

- Hiring a streaker to rush across the fairway at strategic moments

- Training your dog to fetch your opponent's ball

- Bringing a picnic

- Inviting all your friends along to cheer you and boo your opponent

- Sneaking some of those joke exploding golf balls into your opponent's bag

- Bribing onlookers to laugh every time your opponent plays

The uncompromising honesty of the ordinary golfer

The golfer is an honest man.

R&A Rules Committee, 1947

———

Golf is the hardest game in the world to play, and the easiest to cheat at.

Dave Hill

———

Golf has more rules than any other game because golf has more cheaters than any other game.

Bruce Lansky

———

Golf: a game in which you shout 'Fore', shoot six and write down five.

Paul Harvey

———

I once played with a man who cheated so badly that he once had a hole-in-one and wrote down zero on his scorecard.

Bob Bruce

On a recent survey, 80 per cent of golfers admitted cheating. The other 20 per cent lied.

Bruce Lansky

Cheating

Please note this section is not intended to be an instruction manual for aspiring cheats, but a cautionary guide for people who might be cheated by their opponents!

The German writer Bertolt Brecht said that 'if there are obstacles, the shortest line between two points may be the crooked one.' He wasn't talking about golf of course, but crooked golfers everywhere might take those words as an inspiration.

Joke golf balls

Apart from the exploding golf balls mentioned earlier which explode into a cloud of dust on impact, it is also possible to buy several other goofy golf balls with which to astound, confound and amuse fellow players.

You can buy one that once in the air trails out behind it a long party streamer. You can buy a ball that upon impact explodes not in a cloud of dust but in a watery vapour. Then there is the unplayable ball. It has been weighted inside so that it will simply refuse to go in the direction you hit it. These may of course be a joke too far if you are playing in the Open, and they are obviously way beyond the bounds of gamesmanship, but hey, they sound like fun!

The foot wedge

The 'foot wedge' is so well-known in golf circles that one enterprising company has even manufactured a joke foot wedge that attaches to your shoe for maximum propulsion. In reality a 'foot wedge' simply means kicking the ball to a more favourable position when your opponent is not looking.

Sam Snead and the croquet putt

Until something's declared illegal in golf it isn't of course cheating. But if the authorities don't like it and think that it in some way is unfair or not in the spirit of the rules they will ban it. And so it was in the 1960s when Sam Snead started to suffer from the 'yips' while putting, i.e. getting nervous and twitchy. Being the resourceful man he was he invented a new style of putting known as 'croquet putting', where he stood with legs apart with the ball in front of him and hit it croquet style. He even invented a croquet mallet style putter. It worked. He started winning more matches, but then the United States Golf Association (USGA) stepped in and banned the shot in 1968. Legend has it that the great Bobby Jones had seen the shot being played, was appalled, and prompted the USGA to take action.

Creative accounting

Unless you're lucky enough to be playing in a major golf tournament you'll be keeping your own score. This may on occasion lead some players into temptation. Resist it – it's supposed to be a game for gentlemen. And if you can't resist temptation at least don't make your nine-stroke into a hole-in-one.

The non-whiffer

You've probably seen this one played. Your opponent plays a lousy tee shot and then claims that he was just practising his swing. A 'whiffer', as you may know, is a swing that doesn't make contact with the ball. It is then up to you whether you allow him a Mulligan. He is therefore relying on your good sportsmanship without actually displaying any himself.

The magic ball

Your opponent has hit the ball somewhere deep in the woods where the sun don't shine, and he goes off to look for it. To everyone's astonishment, including his own (nominate this man for an Oscar immediately!) he finds the ball just on the edge of the fairway. 'Must have bounced back off a tree.' he mutters nonchalantly. Some bounce, you think to yourself while wondering how that just-muddy ball now looks clean, white and fresh out of the bag.

The dude

Before the ban though, another pro, known as Bob Duden, invented his own croquet style putter with a difference – it was bent! Two thirds down, the shaft bent back towards the player. This putter, named The Dude, became popular but was scuppered by the 1968 ban. Although, interestingly, the ban only applied to shots on the green.

Uncheating

At this point may we humbly introduce the new concept of uncheating? This is where a player is honest to such an exacting degree it actually costs him the match!

The classic example of this was at the 1925 US Open when Bobby Jones was addressing the ball to get out of the rough onto the 11th green when the ball moved slightly. No one else saw it, so the officials left the penalty decision to Jones himself. Jones declared the penalty and lost a stroke. Unfortunately that one stroke was all it took for Jones to ultimately lose the tournament. He was praised for his honesty but simply replied, 'You might as well praise me for not breaking into banks. There is only one way to play this game.'

Could I just check that score card again, sir...

In 1962 Doctor Joseph Boydstone of Bakersfield, California claimed that he had hit 11 aces during the year and 3 during a single round at Bakersfield Country Club.

The record was substantiated by *Golf Digest* although in 1997

Sports Illustrated learnt that Boydstone had many detractors. One of these was Babe Lazane, the retired pro at Bakersfield Country Club, who declared Boydstone 'was a phony'.

Another was Larry Press, who in 1967 was the sports editor of the *Bakersfield Californian* newspaper. Press had Boydstone's hole-in-one records deleted from *The World Almanac*, stating 'there were too many reports that the holes in one were bogus.'

It was also revealed that while Doctor Boydstone may not have been a great golfer, he was a genuinely skilled hypnotist.

If there is any larceny in a man, golf will bring it out.

Paul Gallico

Golf appeals to the idiot in us and the child. Just how childlike golf players become is proven by their frequent inability to count past 5.

It's amazing how people can overcome apparent disabilities

Gordon Ewen, the former President of Western Golf Association recalled how in his youth Bill Murray and his brothers used to caddie for an ageing golfer called Wallace Patterson. Patterson was 'a lovely old guy but about 99 per cent blind.' Since the old man could hardly see, the Murray brothers would 'tell him where his ball went, or where they thought he'd like to hear it went.' While the Murrays were caddying for him, the near blind golfer managed to make three holes in one and collected a handsome trophy each time. 'Eventually,' Gordon Ewen remembered, 'the club caught on and told Bill and his brothers to knock it off!'

Golfing stroke

Going round his local course one afternoon, Harris comes across four other golfers in a bunker. One of the men is lying flat on the ground. His three companions are standing around his body having a fierce argument. 'What on earth's going on?' asks Harris. One of the arguing golfers turns to explain. 'You just wouldn't believe how competitive these bastards are!' he says, 'My golfing partner's just had a stroke and these two are insisting that it's added it to our score.'

Mathematical fact: a man's score at golf is always inversely proportional to the number of people who saw him play.

Angus' new lady friend

Angus meets a new lady member at the golf club one day. Angus and the lady get chatting and end up agreeing to play a round. The new lady member turns out to be an excellent golfer and makes quick work of beating Angus. Not wanting to show any hard feelings, Angus invites her out to dinner. After driving her home, Angus finds himself smooching with his new companion in the front seat of his car. The same thing happens each Sunday for the next four weeks. The lady beats Angus at golf, he takes her out for dinner and they end up kissing and cuddling in his car. On the fourth Sunday Angus suggests they go away for a dirty weekend together, at which point the woman bursts into tears and confesses that she is in fact a transvestite. 'What?!' yells Angus, 'I don't believe anyone could be so dishonest!' 'I'm sorry to have led you on,' says the transvestite. 'It's not that,' says Angus. 'You've been playing off the ladies tee for a whole month!'

Advice for new rule benders

When you start out playing golf you try to learn a few of the basics from golf instructors, from the words of wisdom of professionals or from golfing books. The trouble is you also get advice from people who think that the only way to win is by bending the rules a little bit.

Top Tips For Beginners	Rubbish Tips For Beginners
Stand with feet at shoulder width	Stand on your opponent's toe just as he is about to take his shot
Keep your eye on the ball	Keep your eye on the scorecard for any 'creative accounting'
Keep your knees slightly bent	Keep your caddie slightly bent so he will make sure your ball always stays in play
Keep your head down while driving	Keep your score down by cheating
Have a relaxed grip	Have a relaxed attitude to the scoring of your own shots
Practise your swing	Practise your swearing
Make sure you read the green before putting	Make sure you read the penalties before cheating
Use a sand wedge for a bunker shot	Use an old sandwich as an obstacle to your opponent's line of play

How dangerous can you make a game of golf?

US stunt daredevil Evel Kneivel related how he had had to cut off one of his fingers to fulfil a bet that he had made over a game of golf.

Kneivel claimed that he got tired of one of his golf partners continually cheating. On the 18th hole of one of their games, Kneivel told his opponent, 'I'll bet you $7,000 on this last hole, and if I lose and don't pay up, I'll cut off my finger. And if you lose, you either pay the money or cut off a finger.'

The bet was agreed. Kneivel then hit his shot into a ditch.

'I ended up getting on the green with my fourth shot and making the putt for a 5. Of course, he made birdie. I was so sick of getting cheated by this guy that I said, 'I'm not going to pay you; I'm going to cut off my finger instead.'

Kneivel said he asked to borrow an axe. No axe was available but Kneivel was instead offered 'one of those Boy Scouts shovels that has a hinge and can be turned into an axe.'

Kneiveil being a man of his word allowed the tip to be cut off his finger. As he recalled 'it hurt like hell and there was blood everywhere, but I didn't care back then. The guy I bet was so disgusted he just left. I guess he didn't want the tip of my finger, so I put it in my pocket and headed to a nearby hospital. A doctor sewed it back on, and that was that. Even the nail grew back, although I have this nasty scar now.'

When his partner next wanted a game, Kneivel suggested they played for arms instead.

'He didn't take that bet!' recalled Kneivel.

GAGA GOLF

Golf is a terrible, hopeless addiction, it seems: it makes its devotees willing to trudge miles in any manner of weather, lugging a huge, incommodious and appallingly heavy bag with them, in pursuit of a tiny and fantastically expensive ball, in a fanatical attempt to direct it into a hole the size of a beer glass half a mile away. If anything could be better calculated to convince one of the essential lunacy of the human race, I haven't found it.

Mike Seabrook

He ain't heavy he's my golfing partner

Colin and Angus are out playing a round of golf when Colin suddenly drops dead at the 5th hole. Later that day Angus is mournfully sipping a cocktail at the clubhouse bar when a friend rushes up to offer his condolences. 'I heard you had to carry poor old Angus all the way back to the clubhouse,' says the friend. 'That must have been quite a job.' 'No! Carrying him wasn't difficult at all,' says Angus. 'But I have to admit it was a bit tricky having to put him down at every stroke and then lifting him back up again.'

Clubbed to death

At the golf club bar, Rory and Winston are discussing a recent murder committed by one of their fellow members. 'Did you hear,' asks Rory, 'that Archie Smith beat his wife to death with a five iron?' 'Oh really?' says Winston with sudden interest. 'How many strokes?'

Golf cheat

Pete's wife is suspicious that he's been having an affair and has been using golf as an excuse to go off to another woman every weekend.

'But I have been playing golf,' protests Pete.

'Every weekend for the past ten years?' asks his wife.

'Every weekend!' says Pete firmly.

'I don't believe you,' says his wife, 'You've got some woman tucked away somewhere, and you're just using golf as a cover.'

'All right then,' says Pete, 'come with me then. You can meet all my golfing friends. You can see where we go and what we do.'

So Pete's wife takes him up on the offer and accompanies him to golf games for the next few weeks.

After a couple of months Pete's wife confronts him on the golf course one day in front of all his friends, and slaps him hard round the face.

'You cheating slime bag!' she shouts.

'What do you mean?' protests Pete, 'You've seen me coming to the golf course every weekend. Why do you still not believe me?'

'I'm not stupid, Pete,' she replies, 'No-one could play golf every weekend for ten years and still be as terrible as you are!'

The cruellest game

Golf is not and has never has been a fair game.

Jack Nicklaus

Golf is not just an exercise; it's an adventure, a romance... a Shakespeare play in which disaster and comedy are intertwined.

Harold Segall

Golf is the cruellest game, because eventually it will drag you out in front of the whole school, take your lunch money and slap you around.

Rick Reilly

Golf is like life in a lot of ways. All the biggest wounds are self-inflicted.

Bill Clinton

Golf is more fun than walking naked in a strange place, but not much.

Buddy Hackett

Golf is the cruellest of sports. Like life, it's unfair. It's a harlot. A trollop. It leads you on. It never lives up to its promises. It's a boulevard of broken dreams. It plays with men. And runs off with the butcher.

Jim Murray

Golf is a funny game: one day you're a statue, the next you're a pigeon.

Anon

Golf is essentially an exercise in masochism conducted out of doors.

Paul O'Neill

Golf is a non-violent game played violently from within.

Bob Toski

Golf is not a game. It's bondage. It was obviously devised by a man torn with guilt, eager to atone for his sins.

Jim Murray

Golf is a diabolical game. It's easy to make fun of something that's so bizarre, so painful, so humiliating... yet so joyous.

Ken Green

Golf is the Lord's punishment for man's sins.

James Reston

Just like dad

Damian is a little boy celebrating his sixth birthday. For his birthday party Damian's mum and dad have organized a number of games for him and his friends to play. During a game of skittles against all his little friends from school, Damian steps up to throw his ball but completely misses his shot. Damian grimaces and exclaims, '**** it! ****ing hell! ****ing ****holes! ****ing ****ing **** it!' 'Damian!' gasps his mother, completely astonished at the small boy's outburst. 'Where on earth did you learn language like that?' 'Yes, young man,' his father says sternly, 'you know what little boys who swear when they miss a shot turn into when they grow up?' 'Yes,' says Damian. 'Is it golfers?'

An embarrassing encounter

One day at the golf course Rory and Winston find themselves being held up as they go round while the two women ahead of them continually whiff shots, hunt for lost balls and take an age over every putt. 'I've had enough of this,' says Rory. 'I'm going to go over there and ask those women if we can play through.' And with that Rory strides off towards the two women. A moment later he spins round on his heel and comes straight back to his waiting companion. 'I'm terribly sorry,' explains Rory. 'There's nothing I can do. When I got a bit closer I noticed that one of those women is my wife and the other one is my mistress!' 'That was a close shave!' says Winston. 'Never mind. I'll go over and ask them instead.' And with that Winston strides off towards the two women only to also spin round on his heel a moment later. 'Small world, isn't it?' says Winston sheepishly.

When golf starts to get in the way of work and family, give up work and family.

Golf with the vicar

Angus is playing a round of golf with the vicar. Angus takes his first shot and when he misses, he exclaims in a torrent of terrible language. 'Jesus, Mary and Joseph,' yells Angus, 'God damn it, I missed!' The vicar is taken aback by this outburst. 'Please don't take the name of the Lord in vain again, Angus,' the vicar advises him, 'or God will surely punish you.' Angus takes his second shot. Again he misses and again he cannot control his anger. Under his breath he mutter, 'Jesus effing Christ!' Again the vicar overhears him and chastises him, 'Angus, my son, please refrain from any further blasphemy or I tell you solemnly, the Lord will surely punish you.' The man takes his third shot. Again he misses. He tries biting his lip but in the end it is too much for him and he explodes with another blasphemous outpouring. 'Jesus H Christ I missed again...' he cries out. And at this a bolt of lightning flashes from the heavens. The bolt of lightning misses Angus by three feet and kills the vicar instead. Angus looks up at the storm cloud above his head and hears a booming voice mutter, 'Ahh Jesus Christ! I can't believe I missed...'

Church or golf

George and Hugo regularly meet up for a round of golf on a Sunday morning but then one Sunday, Hugo shows up at the first tee surprisingly late. 'You're late,' says his partner. 'I know,' says Hugo. 'But seeing as it's Sunday morning I thought I better toss a coin to decide whether I should go to church or come here and play golf.' 'OK,' says George. 'But how did that make you quite so late?' 'Well,' explains Hugo, 'in the end I had to make it the best of 97 throws!'

The problem with golf

Golf is the most over-taught and least-learned human endeavour; if they taught sex the way they teach golf, the race would have died out years ago.

Jim Murray

There's no game like golf: you go out with three friends, play 18 holes, and return with three enemies.

Anon

If there is one thing I have learned during my years as a professional, it is that the only thing constant about golf is its inconstancy.

Jack Nicklaus

Golf is assuredly a mystifying game. It would seem that if a person has hit a golf ball correctly a thousand times, he should be able to duplicate the performance at will. But such is certainly not the case.

Bobby Jones

Golf is deceptively simple and endlessly complicated; it satisfies the soul and frustrates the intellect. It is at the same time rewarding and maddening - and it is without a doubt the greatest game mankind has ever invented.

Arnold Palmer

An interesting thing about golf is that no matter how badly you play, it is always possible to get worse.

Anon

Golf is like an 18-year-old girl with big boobs. You know it's wrong but you can't keep away from her.

Val Doonican

The only problem with golf is that the slow people are always in front of you and the fast people always end up behind you.

Anon

Looking on the positive side

Golf is the only game where the worst player gets the best of it. He obtains more out of it as regards both exercise and enjoyment, for the good player gets worried over the slightest mistake, whereas the poor player makes too many mistakes to worry about them.

David Lloyd George

It is more satisfying to be a bad player at golf. The worse you play, the better you remember the occasional good shot.

Nubar Gulbenkian

I shall not so often hear from the King. ... I thank God I am busy with the golfe.

Catherine of Aragon (first wife of King Henry VIII)

Desert island

A man is cast away on a desert island. He survives there alone for ten years until one day an incredibly beautiful woman in a wetsuit emerges from the sea on the same beach. The man runs to greet the first person he has seen in ten years and tells her his story. The woman is astounded. 'Do you mean to say you've been here all this time without having a cigarette?' she asks. 'Oh yes,' says the man. 'In fact I'm desperate for a cigarette.' 'Well,' says the beautiful woman, 'luckily I have a pack here.' And with that she unzips a pocket on her wetsuit and produces a packet of cigarettes. She watches as he enjoys his first cigarette in ten years and asks, 'I bet you'd like a drink of whisky to go with that cigarette?' 'That would be heavenly,' gasps the man. And with that the woman unzips another pocket on her wetsuit and produces a small bottle of whisky. She watches as he savours his drink before remarking, 'Well, I bet there's one other thing you've not been able to enjoy in ten years either. How long is it since you played around?' And with that she starts to unzip the front of her wetsuit. 'Good God!' says the man. 'You're not going to tell me you've got a set of golf clubs in there as well?'

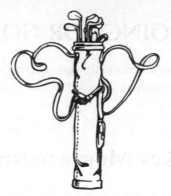

Is there a aoctor
on the course?

Alfie and his wife Poppy are out playing golf. They get to the
sixth hole, when Poppy suddenly falls to the ground suffering a
heart attack. 'Quick! Go and get help! Go and call the doctor to
come out here!' she gasps, before passing out. Alfie dutifully trots
off to the club house to phone for the doctor. Half an hour later
Poppy regains consciousness only to find she is still lying on the
golf course while her husband lines up a shot. 'What's going on?'
she asks. 'Didn't you call the doctor out?' 'Of course I have, dear,'
replies Alfie. 'He's already on the fourth hole.' 'The fourth hole?'
says Poppy. 'But this is an emergency!' 'Don't panic!' says her
husband. 'He'll be here as soon as he can. The people on the fifth
hole are letting him play through.'

Golf in the afterlife?

When golfer and coach Abe Mitchell died in 1936 at the age of 77
he was buried with his favourite five-iron.

GOING FOR GOLF

I'm going to win so much money this year, my caddie will make the top 20 money-winners list.

Lee Trevino

A Mickey Mouse tournament?

In 1971 a new PGA event was inaugurated: The Walt Disney World Open Invitational, and the first winner was, arguably the greatest golf player ever, Jack Nicklaus. He also went back to win it in 1972 and 1973, by which time it had been renamed The Walt Disney World Golf Classic. The tournament ran right up to 2006 when it was superseded by the Children's Miracle Network Classic, still played at Orlando in Florida. The prize money purse in 2009 was $4.7 million, with the winner Stephen Ames getting $846,000. Definitely not a Mickey Mouse tournament then.

The Ryder Cup

Samuel Ryder must have been a big golfing fan to provide the cup for one of golf's most important tournaments. But was he? Samuel Ryder had reached the age of 50 before he ever set foot on a golf course, and only then at the suggestion of a friend who thought the fresh air might help him recover from an illness. Ryder wasn't too sure about the idea; he was after all, more of a cricket fan.

But in 1927 the first Ryder Cup was played between a USA team and one from Britain and Ireland. By the 1970s the Americans were dominating the tournament so much that it was agreed that the British team would become the European team, taking in players from the whole continent, and since then the tournament wins have been more evenly spread.

911 and The Ryder Cup

The Ryder Cup was played biennially on odd numbered years (apart from during the Second World War) until 2001, when the terrorist attacks on America on September 11 meant the tournament was delayed until 2002, since when it has been played on even numbered years.

Who's that on The Ryder Cup?

The Ryder Cup is named after Samuel Ryder who bought the £250 prize gold cup for the winner of the first tournament in 1927, but the likeness of the man depicted on it is not of Samuel Ryder, but a depition of his golf coach Abe Mitchell. Samuel Ryder employed him at what was then the enormous cost of £1,000 a year.

Some of the World's weirder golf trophies

A trophy in the form of a large clam is given to the winner of the Qatar Masters.

The prize in the Northern Telecom Open used to be a Spanish Conquistador's Helmet.

The Bay Hill Invitational subsequently re-dubbed the Arnold Palmer Invitational awards its winner with a Giant Sword.

Thuashni Selvaratnam won the 1989 Sri Lankan Ladies Amateur Open Golf Championship. Thuashni was born in June 1976. She won the championship aged just 12 years 324 days.

Open records

Harry Vardon won the British Open on 6 occasions: 1896, 1898, 1899, 1903, 1911 and 1914. James Braid won 5 times in 1901, 1905, 1906, 1908 and 1910, as did J H Taylor in 1894, 1895, 1900, 1909 and 1913. J H Taylor also holds the record for the longest span between British Open victories with his final win coming 19 years after his first. The runner-up for this record is Harry Vardon with 18 years between his 1896 and 1914 wins. Taylor and Vardon are also, with Gary Player, the only players to have won in three decades.

Clearly competition has become more marked since those days. Nevertheless in more recent decades Peter Thomson was champion in 1954, 1955, 1956, 1958 and 1965 while Tom Watson won in 1975, 1977, 1980, 1982 and 1983. Jack Nicklaus holds the record for coming second in the British Open which he has done on seven occasions: 1964, 1967, 1968, 1972, 1976, 1977 and 1979.

Even more out in the Open

Four golfers have won the US Open on four occasions:

Willie Anderson in 1901, 1903, 1904 and 1905
Bobby Jones in 1923, 1926, 1929 and 1930
Ben Hogan in 1948, 1950, 1951 and 1953
Jack Nicklaus in 1962, 1967, 1972 and 1980

The Tooting Bec Cup

The one golfing trophy that most non-golfers will have heard of is the Ryder Cup but one wonders how many realize that there is a prestigious golfing trophy bearing the name of Tooting – home of legendary TV character Citizen Smith?

Back in 1901 there was a golf links on Tooting Bec Common, and a 36-hole stroke play tournament was inaugurated. The prize was of course the Tooting Bec Cup but that inaugural year of 1901 was the first and last time it was contested there. Over the next eight years the tournament was played at various venues from Romford to Neasden. Then in 1910 it became a qualifying tournament for the News of The World Matchplay Championship. Since 1924 the Tooting Bec Cup has been awarded to the PGA player (born in UK or Republic of Ireland, or with parents who were) who records the lowest score in the British Open. Over the years it has gone to some of the greatest names in golf such as Tony Jacklin, Nick Faldo, Sandy Lyle and Colin Montgomerie. Power to the people of Tooting!

The Bob Jones Award

This award, which was started in 1955 by the United States Golf Association (USGA), is awarded in recognition for distinguished sportsmanship in golf. Many of the great players such as Jack Nicklaus and Gary Player have won the award but in 2008 an ex-president won it! George Bush senior was only the second non-career golfer to win the award. In 1978 the award had gone jointly to Bob Hope and Bing Crosby. The award was named in honour of golfer Bobby Jones. Presumably 'Bob' was felt to be a more suitable name for an award than 'Bobby'!

Union golfer

The union members are all out on strike and negotiations with their employers are at a delicate stage. An impasse has been caused by the employers accusing the workers of flagrantly abusing their sick leave entitlement. 'That's an outrageous suggestion,' says the union leader, 'what proof have you got?' And with that the managing director holds up last week's edition of the local newspaper. 'Look at the sports page!' he declares. 'There's a photograph of one of our employees holding up the trophy in a semi-professional golf tournament. It seems he won seven under par on the very same day he called in sick and unable to come in to work!' The union negotiator has to think quickly before breaking the silence. 'Yes,' says the negotiator, 'and just think what sort of score this man could have got if he hadn't been on his deathbed at the time!'

GOLFING GRATES

You can't call it a sport. You don't run, jump, you don't shoot, you don't pass. All you have to do is buy some clothes that don't match.

Steve Sax

Golf! You hit down to make the ball go up. You swing left and the ball goes right. The lowest score wins. And on top of that, the winner buys the drinks!

Anon

People who say golf is fun are probably the same people who rationalize the game by saying they play it for their health. What could be fun about a game in the entire history of which nobody has ever shot the score he thought he should have?

Charles Price

Golf is a game invented by the same people who think that's music coming out of a set of bagpipes.

Anon

A wife's fury

Ben is an avid golfer. One Saturday he is putting his clubs in the back of the car ready for his regular weekend outing to the local club. Suddenly his wife appears at the door looking furious. 'Do you know what?' she screams at him. 'If you offered to spend a weekend here at home with me instead of going out golfing, I'd probably drop dead with shock!' Ben considers this for a moment before replying. 'Do you know what?' he yells back at her. 'If you'd said 'definitely' rather than 'probably', I might have considered it!'

No golf please we're Ukrainian!

According to *Golf Digest* the most populous countries in the world where no evidence of golf could be found are:

Ukraine (population 47,732,079)
Sudan (39,148,162)
Yemen (20,024,867)
Mali (11,956,788)
Belarus (10,310,520)

Claims and counter claims

Hard though it may be to believe, not everyone likes golf. So, what are the main complaints? And how can you answer these naysayers?

CLAIM	ANSWER
It's boring	Have you ever watched televized chess?
It's only for middle-aged white males	Tiger Woods
It takes up beautiful open spaces	If there weren't a golf-course there do you think someone would go out and water the grass every morning?
Men go off and leave their wives for days at a time	So do plenty of other men – and they're not playing golf!
Women are excluded from the men's game	Rubbish! Nick Faldo once had a female caddie – called Fanny
It's elitist	You're only saying that because you can't get into your local golf club
It's full of weird jargon	So is computing. We have birdies, you have tweets – what's your beef?
I don't understand the rules	Join the club!
It takes too long	Compared with test cricket it's over in a flash

Golf is the most useless outdoor game ever devised to waste time and try the sprit of man.

Westbrook Pegler

There is one thing in this world that is dumber than playing golf. That is watching someone else playing golf. What do you actually get to see? Thirty-seven guys in polyester slacks squinting at the sun. Doesn't that set your blood racing?

Peter Andrews

Any game where a man of 60 can beat a man of 30 ain't no game.

Burt Shotten

If you want to take long walks, take long walks. If you want to hit things with sticks, hit things with sticks. But there's no excuse for combining the two and putting the results on TV. Golf is not so much a sport as an insult to lawns.

National Lampoon

THE GOOD, THE BAD
AND THE UNLIKELY

What's in a name?

When you first go out on a golf course, you're obviously a bit apprehensive. What if you execute the perfect swing only to find that afterwards that your ball is still sitting doggedly on the tee? What if you whack the ball into the trees or into the water and never see it again? What if you get hit by a golf ball? The game of golf is fraught with potential disasters waiting to happen.

So spare a thought for those poor souls who turned out in Shasta County, California for the American Red Cross Golf Tournament in May 2009 only to find it was sponsored by Cronic Disaster services. They are actually specialists in fire and water damage restoration though you can forgive a novice golfer feeling slightly nervous on hearing the name of the sponsor. Nice to know though that the Red Cross are on hand in the event that you are concussed by a stray ball!

Dangers of lost balls

Hunting for lost balls can sometimes result in bramble pricks, nettle stings, snake bites, bee stings and many other hazards, but in 1996 a golfer paid the ultimate price for losing a lost ball. He was playing at Caddockstown golf course in County Kildare, Northern Ireland when his ball went into a ditch. He went to retrieve it and had the unpleasant experience of a rat running up his trouser leg. He managed to extricate the rodent, but is believed to have contracted Weil's disease from it, which later killed him.

Dangers of flying balls

It has been estimated that the air speed of a golf ball can be up to 150mph (significantly less after it has hit the ground) and every year people are killed by flying golf balls. There seem to be no accurate figures for the number of people killed each year by golf balls, but in addition to the people killed, birds, foxes and squirrels have also been victims of this danger.

Dangers of golf buggies

In addition to the dangers posed by flying golf balls players need also to be careful when using golf buggies. In 2007, 65 year-old Edward Payne died when his golf buggy went over a ridge at the Pala Mesa Resort golf club in San Diego USA. There have been several other deaths reported of people falling from golf buggies or being run over by them.

Moose on the loose

In June 2005 golfers at Veterans Memorial Golf Course, Walla Walla, Washington found an unexpected hazard. A female moose had settled beneath a tree at the 3rd hole. The moose was herded across the fairways and off the by State Fish and Wildlife officers. Clearly the moose had turned out to not be a paid up member of the club.

Mass lightning strike

In a single event in June 2005, 19 golfers were struck by lightning in the town of Kremmling, Colorado.

The golfers were participating in what was termed the Fourth Annual Kremmling Cliff Classic Golf Tournament. This was not however a tournament played according to the strict official rules of the game. Instead it was played on the edge of a cliff a mile or so from the town. The aim of the competition was to hit balls off the top of the cliff as close as possible to targets in the valley below.

When the lightning approached, the golfers sheltered in their cars. They emerged when they believed the storm had passed and made their way back towards the cliff edge. The lightning then struck again and arced through 19 players. One of them described how he had at first felt 'totally paralyzed' before feeling a surge of pain and heat as though he was on fire. Another said he had felt 'a dead feeling' from his chest down. A third said, 'It felt like someone hit me over the head with a baseball bat.'

One of the golfers, Gary Almgren, later related his experience: 'When the lightning bolt hit me, it stopped my heart. I was incredibly lucky, because a nurse was up there. She and the fire fighters saved my life by giving me CPR for about 20 minutes. The lightning collapsed my lungs, blew out my right eardrum and heated the cell phone in my pocket so much that it burned my leg. I also had burn blisters on my hands in the shape of a golf grip. It took me more than six months to get back in shape, but

I'm starting to feel good. The only scars I have are the two little marks on my leg where the lightning exited my body.'

Fifteen of the men suffered minor injuries and four were taken to hospital. Fortunately however all the cliff top golfers survived the strike.

The number of people injured in the Kremmling valley as a result of golf balls fired from the cliff above them was not reported!

Golf streakers

As if you haven't got enough to put you off your game what with low-flying birds, insects, rain, wind and hail, and if you're a pro, press photographers, crowds, autograph hunters, and spectators' phones ringing, you may also have to contend with streakers. Unless you are a pro you are unlikely to be troubled by such an interruption to your concentration, but if you're Tiger Woods you're probably going to have to get used to it.

Although the word 'streaker' has got a strong hint of the 1970s about it, the phenomenon has been going on regularly ever since Britain's first ever streaker raced across the rugby pitch at Twickenham in 1974.

Serial British streaker Mark Roberts has done his thing at hundreds of sporting events including three British Opens and one Ryder Cup.

During the British Open at Royal Troon in 1997 a female streaker wearing nothing but some tiger's ears and body and face paint imitating tiger's stripes ran onto the 18th green at the end of the match. Wonder who she was supporting?

Two years later, another female streaker, clearly another fan of Tiger Woods, dashed on to the course at Carnoustie during the

British Open to give her hero a kiss. Despite at least having the decency to keep her underwear on, she was fined. (Streaking is still against the law).

But streakers are ever inventive. At the 2006 Ryder Cup held at the K club, Straffan in Northern Ireland a male streaker appeared at the 18th green and dived into the lake. Unfortunately he did so just as J.J. Henry was about to putt for the American team. Paul McGinley, who was playing for Europe, promptly conceded the 25-foot putt, although Europe had already won. Had Henry played the putt and missed though, Europe would have won an even greater, indeed record, victory over the Americans.

So that's where your ball went

In 2005 a pair of storks decided to nest at Golf Park Krogaspe near Neumuenster. They settled by the 200-metre mark on the driving range, a fairly remote area where they did not get disturbed. Storks are rarely known to build their nests on the ground so this was unusual behaviour for starters. The storks were however a noticeably eccentric pair as they then took to filling their nest with stolen golf balls but failed to hatch any of them out. As this was a slightly sad situation, conservationists planted a genuine egg salvaged from another nest. The storks accepted the real egg along with their golf balls and a chick was hatched a few days later.

Most famous death
on a golf course

On October 14, 1977 Bing Crosby played a round of gold with some friends in Madrid. Unfortunately, straight afterwards he suffered a heart attack and died. His often reported last words were: 'That was a great game of golf, fellers.' However, one source claims that those weren't actually his very last words. After that he is reported to have said, 'Let's go and get a Coke.'

Incidentally, Bing's son, Nathaniel was the youngest winner of the US Amateur golf Championship in 1981 at the age of 19. The record stood until 1994 when it was won by some new guy called Tiger Woods... whatever happened to him?

Bing Crosby is also the singer of the most famous song ever about golf. 'Straight Down the Middle' was written by the celebrated songwriters Sammy Cahn and Jimmy Van Heusen, and Crosby's recording even starts with the shout 'Fore!'

What could be more Scottish?

Whistling Straits golf course in Kohler, Wisconsin was the scene of the 2004 PGA Championships. Whistling Straits resembles one of the great courses of Scotland. The TV company providing coverage of the championships therefore had the bright idea of filming a lone bagpiper playing on the course. This would surely add a touch of atmosphere to their coverage's opening sequence!

Andy Willett, an accountant from Delavan, Wisconsin was the amateur piper who was employed to stroll across the links at sunset dressed in full Scottish regalia.

According to Andy, 'We filmed at one location about two-thirds of the way down the 13th fairway. I didn't know it then, but there was a hidden championship tee box about 250 yards from where I was standing.

'It's a blind shot for the golfer, and we didn't know to check if anyone was there. I heard 'Fore!' and my first reaction was to raise my hand to cover my face. Unfortunately, it was too late.'

A ball hit Andy above his eye. A few moments later, blood began pouring down his face. It must have looked like some terrible moment from the Jacobite rebellion!

The film crew put the injured piper on the back of a golf cart and drove him back to the club house.

According to Andy, 'You couldn't get an ambulance out to the 13th hole, and they usually don't allow regular golf carts on the course, so the trails are pretty rough. I was bouncing all over the place, and it took 20 minutes to get back.'

'Luckily,' he said of his injury, 'I'd been wearing a Glengarry hat made from 100 percent Scottish wool. I think the ball hit the rim, which probably saved me from a massive head injury. I also had a pretty nasty bruise on my index finger.'

So clearly some people will do anything to stop people playing the bagpipes.

Evel Kneivel + a golf buggy: what could possibly happen next...

In the 1970s US daredevil stunt driver Evel Kneivel used to play golf at the Rivermont course in Alpharetta, Georgia. One day the frustrations of the game led Mr Kneivel to attempt an ill advised jump in his golf buggy.

He recalled how the 17th hole at Rivermont was a par 3 and 'steeply downhill'.

'The path has a series of hairpin turns, and if you ignore them you'll just keep going over a huge ledge. The guys I hung out with down there pointed out that if you gathered enough speed you could go over the cliff and land where the path resumes farther down the hill. For days they dared me to make the jump, and when I came to the hole in a foul mood one afternoon – I wasn't playing well – I just went for it.'

Halfway down the hill Kneivel realized he had made a mistake. 'You have no idea how unstable a three-wheel golf cart is when it becomes airborne.' Nevertheless he managed a perfect landing. The tyres on the buggy were however 'like basketballs, and the cart bounced like an SOB.'

Kneivel recalled how when he finally managed to stop the buggy he immediately got a 'royal chewing out' from his wife who had been one of his passengers.

The moral of the story: it was never wise to accept a lift with Evel Kneivel.

Freak golfing eye accident

In February 2009 in a freak accident, Irish golfer John Morrison lost an eye after being hit with his own ball. Morrison had been playing the second hole of the Jack's Point course near Queenstown on New Zealand's South Island.

His shot caused his ball to strike a rock, bounce back and hit him in the face. The ball shattered Morrison's spectacles causing shards of the broken lens to penetrate his left eye.

Lightning strike
at The Western Open

The worst lightning strike during a professional golf tournament occurred in June 1975 at the Western Open at Butler National Golf Club in Chicago.

Play had been suspended and current PGA champion Lee Trevino was sitting with a young player, Jerry Heard, near a pond by the 15th green sheltering under an umbrella. A spectator described seeing Trevino roll over a couple of times. At first she thought he had done this as a joke but he then cried out, 'I've been hit.' Both Trevino and Heard had been struck by lightning. It was later suggested that the bolt had gone through their clubs and into their bodies.

At the same time fellow golfer Bobby Nichols was on the first fairway with Tony Jacklin and Jim Ahern. Jacklin and Ahern reported a minor strike. Jacklin commented, 'I don't know if I was hit. I was standing about 15 yards from Bobby and I was holding a club and all of a sudden a tingle went through me and I wasn't holding the club.'

Similarly Arnold Palmer on the 14th fairway had been about to swing but suddenly found the club flying from his hands.

Nichols, Jacklin recalled, seemed all right although shaken up and they ran for cover with Jim Ahern.

'There was another bolt while we were running,' Jacklin continued, 'and Bobby bent over and put his arms over his head and ducked down.

Jacklin and Ahern did not require treatment but Trevino, Heard and Nichols were all taken to the intensive care unit of Hinsdale Hospital. There the doctor attending them commented that it was 'quite phenomenal' that they had survived and suggested that the lightning might have hit the water and bounced resulting in the golfers not suffering a direct hit.

Trevino was reported to have a burn across his back where the lightning had exited from his body. He later described the sensation of being struck: 'When I got hit, it was like being hit by two ball-peen hammers on the ears. It was a nice warm feeling. Evidently I was gone, then I woke up in the hospital and I was in pain.' He later joked, 'If you are caught on a golf course during a storm and are afraid of lightning,' he later quipped, 'hold up a 1-iron. Not even God can hit a 1-iron.'

Trevino was 35 years old when he was struck at the 1975 Western Open. He recovered to win another 9 PGA Tour events although he did suffer severe back problems which some attributed to the strike.

'How can they beat me?' he quipped subsequently. 'I've been struck by lightning, had two back operations, and been divorced twice.'

In a storm during the first round of the 1991 US Open a lightning strike killed one spectator and injured five others. The six men had sheltered from the storm under a willow tree near the 11th tee of the Hazeltine National Golf Club. The man who was killed was a 27-year-old whose death was attributed to cardiac arrest. The death of the spectator was believed to be the first ever caused by lightning at a championship golf tournament in the USA.

Crowned by a seven iron

Prince William revealed he had been injured on a golf course. As a result the heir to the British throne now sports what he calls a 'Harry Potter scar':

> *'I call it that because it glows sometimes and some people notice it – other times they don't notice it at all. We were on a putting green; the next thing you know there was a seven-iron and it came out of nowhere and it hit me in the head.'*

A man's got to do what he's got to do

Dudley gets home one evening and finds his wife in her shortest sexiest nightie waiting for him in the bedroom. 'Hello, darling,' she whispers nibbling his ear and producing a set of handcuffs, 'I thought for a treat I would let you do something a bit kinky.' 'Fantastic!' says Dudley taking the handcuffs and locking her wrists to the bedstead. 'OK,' purrs his wife, 'now you can do whatever you want.' 'Really?' says Dudley with glee before running out of the bedroom, throwing his clubs in the back of the car and driving off at high speed to the golf course.

HIS AND HERS

When I die, bury me on the golf course so my husband will visit.

Anon

What male golfers say about female golfers (and vice versa)

Him: Of course women are all right on the putting green, but they can't drive a ball 300 yards.
Her: Of course men can hit the ball further; they don't have to do a stack of washing and ironing before they go out on the golf course.

Him: There's nothing wrong with women playing golf – as long as it's not at my club.
Her: I wouldn't dream of playing at my husband's club – he'd hate it if I did better than him.

Him: The only women you should have in a golf club are the ones working behind the bar.
Her: The only reason my husband joined his golf club was because he thought I couldn't join and he could chat up the women behind the bar!

Him: For women, golf is another excuse for shopping, as if they needed one – new outfits, accessories…
Her: For men, golf is just another excuse to spend time away from their wives, as if they needed one – drinking, talking business…

Him: If God had meant women to play golf he would have made them better at it.
Her: If God had meant men to play golf she would have made them better at it.

Him: Can you imagine any amateur female player getting as good as Tiger Woods?
Her: Can you imagine any amateur male player getting as good as Michelle Wie?

Him: Golf was invented by men, so it's a man's game. End of story.
Her: Golf was invented by men wearing skirts so what's wrong with it being played by women wearing trousers?

Him: If women spent as much time practicing their swing as they do on choosing what to wear on the golf course then I might take them a bit more seriously.
Her: If men spent as much time choosing what to wear on the golf course as they do on practicing their swing I might take them a bit more seriously.

Any old iron

Two women are talking about their respective husbands' new love of golf. 'It drives me nuts,' says the first woman. 'Every weekend he's out on the course come rain or shine. I never see him.' 'To be honest,' says the second, 'I was delighted when my husband took up golf.' 'Why?' asks the first woman, mystified. 'It was the first time I'd ever seen him use an iron!'

New golfer

One Sunday morning, Rory is complaining to his golfing partner, Winston, that his wife has also recently taken up the game.

'I wish she'd never taken up golf,' huffs Rory. 'Between you and me, she is spending so much time practicing that she's cut our sex life down to just once a month.' 'Count yourself lucky, old man,' replies his friend. 'She's cut some of us out altogether.'

How long can it take?

A blushing bride comes down the aisle but when she reaches the altar, she notices her groom is standing there with his golf bag and clubs at his side. She hisses to him under her breath, 'Why have you brought your golf clubs with you?' 'Well,' he says, 'this isn't going to take all day, is it?'

The love of golf

What is love compared with holing out before your opponent?

P.G. Wodehouse

Golf is like love. One day you think you are too old and the next day you want to do it again.

Roberto de Vicenzo

It is nevertheless a game of considerable passion, either of the explosive type, or that which burns inwardly and sears the soul.

Bobby Jones

Golf is very much like a love affair. If you don't take it seriously, it's no fun, if you do, it breaks your heart. Don't break your heart, but flirt with the possibility.

Louise Suggs

The golf swing is like sex: you can't be thinking of the mechanics of the act while you're doing it.

Dave Hill

Golf and sex are the only things you can enjoy without being good at them.

Jimmy DeMaret

Dan would rather play golf than have sex any day.

Marilyn Quayle (wife of former US Vice President Dan Quayle)

Golf is a lot like sex. It's something you can enjoy all your life. And if you remain an amateur, you get to pick your own playing partners.

Jess Sweetser

Love and putting are mysteries for the philosopher to solve. Both subjects are beyond golfers.

Tommy Armour

Tennis is like a wonderful, longstanding relationship with

a husband. Golf is a tempestuous, lousy lover; it's totally
unpredictable, a constant surprise.

Dinah Shore

Give me golf clubs, fresh air and a beautiful partner, and you can
keep the clubs and the fresh air.

Jack Benny

A wife's final warning

One day at the golf course, Rory is looking rather melancholy. He
tells his golfing partner Winston that his wife has threatened to
leave him if he doesn't give up golf. 'That's terrible,' says Winston.
'What are you going to do?' 'Well,' says Rory, 'I'm certainly going
to miss her.'

A demanding round

Chester gets a ransom demand for his wife. The note says to bring
£50,000 in used notes to the 17th hole of the local golf club, the
following day at noon or he will never see his wife again. And
so the next day Chester gathers the money together in a suitcase
and sets off to the golf course. Unfortunately he does not turn
up at the 17th hole until half past two in the afternoon. When
he eventually arrives the kidnappers emerge from behind a bush
looking furious. 'You idiot,' say the kidnappers, 'we told you to
be here at midday! We ought to cut your wife's ears off for this!'
'Hey!' says Chester. 'Give me a break. My driver broke on the
second hole, and I lost a ball on the 15th...'

Anniversary confession

Ageing married couple Alfie and Poppy are celebrating their golden wedding anniversary when Alfie asks Poppy if she has ever been unfaithful to him. Poppy bites her lip and tells her husband, 'Just three times.' 'I suppose three times isn't so bad over 50 years,' considers Alfie. 'When did it first happen?' 'Well,' says Poppy, 'remember that time you needed money to start up your business and no-one would give you any? I had to sleep with the local bank manager to get him to grant you a loan.' 'You made that sacrifice for me?' asks Alfie. 'How wonderful of you! When was the second time?' 'Well,' says Poppy, 'Remember that operation you needed that no-one would perform because it was too dangerous? I had to sleep with the surgeon at the local hospital to get him to do it.' 'My goodness,' says Alfie! 'Your action saved my life! When was the third time?' 'Well,' says Poppy. 'Remember that time you wanted to be President of the Golf Club and you were 52 votes short..?'

History repeats

Husband and wife golfers Benjy and Maisie are enjoying a game of golf when Benjy hits a shot that lands in the doorway of a greenhouse next to the course. Maisie holds the greenhouse door open for her husband but he misjudges his swing and knocks her on the head with his club killing her instantly. Several years later Benjy is back on the same golf course with his new wife, Bella. He slices the same shot and, again, the ball lands in the doorway of the greenhouse next to the course. Bella asks, 'Do you want me to hold the door open for you, dear?' 'No thank you,' replies Benjy. 'I tried a very similar shot a few years ago and I ended up taking a triple bogie.'

Re-kindling the passion

Poppy and her husband Alfie realize the passion seems to have faded from their relationship and so they decide to visit a marriage counsellor. After a number of sessions Poppy and Alfie don't feel that they are making any progress at re-kindling their desire for one other. The counsellor is so frustrated to hear this that he decides to make a graphic demonstration to try and get some reaction out of Alfie. He grabs Poppy and starts kissing and fondling her all over. 'There, you see!' he tells Alfie. 'This is what your wife needs. You need to do this kind of thing every Monday, Wednesday, Saturday and Sunday. What have you got to say to that?' 'Well,' says Alfie, 'I can bring her in to you on Mondays and Wednesdays but Saturdays and Sundays are my golf days.'

Gentle exercise

Avid young golfer Chris and his wife go to their pre-natal class. Their instructor tells them about doing plenty of gentle exercise during pregnancy.

'Don't forget,' says the instructor, 'at this stage in your pregnancy a long slow walk is ideal exercise. And for a bit of company, why not take your partner with you.'

'That sounds a great idea,' says Chris, 'but do you think in her condition she'd be able to carry my golf bag?'

Indulging his passion

Alfie arrives home late one night and his wife, Poppy, is not pleased. She demands to know where he has been until this time and Alfie tells her, 'I was on my way to the golf club this morning but I saw a beautiful 20-year-old girl stuck at the side of the road with a flat tyre. So what was I supposed to do? I stopped the car, I helped fix her tyre and she was so grateful she invited me back to her place for a drink and after a little while one thing led to another and we ended up in her bedroom, tearing each other's clothes off and making mad passionate love for the rest of the day and night.'

Poppy listens to all this and looks her husband over. 'You lying bastard!' she yells at him. 'You've been out at the golf course all day, haven't you?'

Dudley's obsession

Dudley becomes obsessed by golf and takes every opportunity to sneak in a game. Every Sunday he is up at six o'clock so he can be first out on the local course. One Sunday however, he kisses his wife goodbye and sets off in his car only to find the weather is absolutely appalling. He reaches the golf course only to hear the weather forecast on the radio telling him that severe thunderstorms are expected all day. As the weather is clearly not going to improve, Dudley reluctantly turns his car around and drives back home. By the time he gets back, it's still only seven o'clock. He figures that his wife will still be asleep, so he creeps upstairs, tiptoes into the bedroom, slips his clothes off and slides into bed next to her.

His wife says sleepily, 'Morning, my darling.'

'Morning, dear,' whispers Dudley. 'The weather's terrible outside.'

'I know,' replies his wife. 'And can you believe my idiot husband is out in it playing golf right now!'

GOLF LINGO

"Fore!"

Angus is on the golf course playing against a friend of his who happens to be a city trader. The city trader is looking forward to the game even though he has never played before and knows nothing about golf. Angus tees off and shouts, 'Fore!' Without thinking the city trader immediately yells in response, 'Three ninety-five!'

The origins of the lingo explained

Bogie
To the golfer of course this means going one over par, but rather unpleasantly it also has associations with nasal mucus and ghostly bogeymen. Simply, it means something unpleasant or unwanted, perhaps even slightly scary. It is thought to come from the Scottish word 'bogle', another word for a goblin or ghost.

Bunker
This comes from the same root as 'bunk' as in a bed on board ship. So it meant a hole or a recess, and then came to mean a receptacle as in 'coal bunker'.

Caddie/caddy
Scotland's claim to have invented the game or at least, to have popularized it, can be given some weight by the fact that some of

the terms used in golf come from the land of bagpipes and haggis. In 18th century Scotland 'caddie' meant a messenger or porter, and was short for 'cadet'. It has also been claimed that the usage came originally from Mary Queen of Scots' playing of the game in France where she used military cadets as caddies.

I don't think anywhere is there a symbiotic relationship between caddie and player like there is in golf.

Johnny Miller

Club
Many a merry quip has been based on the dual meaning of 'golf club' but if you go back far enough 'club' meaning a stick with a heavy end, and 'club' meaning a gaggle of people who have joined together meant the same thing. 'Club' came from 'clump' which meant a cluster. So it is a stick with a knobbly cluster of lumps and bumps at one end, and a cluster of people. Not a lot of people know that.

Fairway
Originally used in relation to a river, meaning an easily navigable central part away from the weeds, sandy banks and other hazards. Quite appropriate then.

Fore!
Old term meaning 'look in front of you!'; 'fore' meaning 'front'.

Links
Why is a golf course sometimes know as 'the links'? 'Links' originally meant grassy open (usually flat) land by the seaside

which was a popular place to play. Since then it has become almost synonymous with 'golf course'. In fact the first golf courses are believed to have been along the stretch of Scottish coast between Dunbar and Leith.

Mulligan
A second tee shot that might be allowed by some kindly opponent after a disastrous first shot. Origin unknown, but is it a coincidence that in the USA 'mulligan stew' is one made up of scraps?

Putt
Again, a Scottish term. 'Putt' is simply the Scottish version of 'put', so a player would really be attempting to 'put' the ball in the hole.

Scratch player
One with no handicap. The 'scratch' part means a starting point and probably comes from boxing where a scratch or mark was scored into the ground showing where the fighters should stand at the start of their bout.

Shag
Meaning to retrieve practice balls. 'shag' means rough as in 'shaggy' so this probably comes from the fact that the retrieved balls are a bit rough and ready.

Stroke
Why is it called a stroke when quite often a golf shot is far from gentle as this word implies? In this case 'stroke' comes from 'struck' a far more appropriately forceful word when one is trying to whack the ball 400 yards.

Making an ash of it

Old Bert has been playing golf all his life and he requests in his will that his ashes be scattered over the 18th green at his golf club.

When he dies his widow brings the ashes along and goes to check with the club's fussy secretary that Bert's wishes can be carried out.

'Well, it's highly irregular of course,' he replies, 'but Bert was one of our longest standing members, so I suppose we could allow it. But instead of scattering the ashes all over the green, could you just pour them down the hole?'

'Well,' says his widow uncertainly, 'I suppose so. I expect he'd have been happy ending up there anyway.'

So Bert's widow, the club officials and some of Bert's old golfing chums gather round the 18th and Bert's widow tips the urn upside down over the hole.

Suddenly there is a strong gust of wind, and the ashes are blown a few inches from the hole. This leaves Bert's widow clearly distraught.

Sid, one of Bert's old golfing chums, puts a comforting arm round the widow's shoulder and says 'Don't you worry about it, love. We understand, you're bound to be upset, given the circumstances. Have a mulligan on us!'

Birdies

An albatross and an eagle are flying over a golf course when the eagle says, 'Do you know they've named a golf shot after me?'

'Yes, I had heard that,' replies the albatross haughtily, 'but they've named one after me too and it's a much better shot.'

'Really?' replies the eagle, 'so you're saying the eagle is a common shot are you?'

'Well, it's more common than an albatross,' says the albatross, 'but to be perfectly fair to you, the commonest shot of all is named after a bird I've never heard of.'

'Which one is that?' asks the eagle.

'The 'Ohbuggeriveslice tit!'

Calling the shots

It's a mystery why golf shots are named after birds, though yes, they do fly across the green, but then so do butterflies and we don't have a Red Admiral shot or a Grizzled Skipper shot do we? The ones that most golfers will know, but perhaps will never actually attain are:

Birdie – One under par for one hole
Eagle – Two under par for one hole
Albatross – Three under par for one hole
Condor – Four under par for one hole

But what is the term for a five under par? Do you think you're ever going to need to know that? Do you think anyone's ever going to need to know that? In theory, it's possible to get a five under par by getting a hole-in-one on a par six hole, but the possibility of that happening is so remote that they haven't yet come up with a term for it. Perhaps though, we should have one on standby just in case.

To suit the shot it would need to be something amazing, awe-inspiring, huge, legendary, and frankly a bit unlikely and rather frightening... how about the Pterodactyl?

Names for extraordinary shots though are all very well but surely it's time for some new names for the shots that most ordinary golfers are more likely to experience.

Ostrich: one that buries itself in the sand.
Dodo: one that disappears without trace.
Pigeon: one that drops on somebody's head.
Woodpecker: one that drives straight into a tree.
Emu: one that never gets off the ground.
Heron: one that heads straight for the water.
Reed Warbler: one that disappears into the long grass.
Phoenix: fabulous, mythical, and never seen, but often talked about.
Orville: one that annoys you for days afterwards.

... And some more definitions

Fairway: a narrow strip of mown grass that separates 2 groups of golfers looking for lost balls in the rough.
Follow-through: the part of the swing that takes place after the ball has been hit, but before the club has been thrown.
Caddie: a golfer's gopher.
A slice with jam: a mis-hit that somehow lands on the green.
A hole-in-one: an event that makes a blue moon look commonplace.

Iron: something a wife uses for pressing clothes and a husband uses for pressing engagements.

Golf buggy: the only perfect drive you're likely to see all day

---

If it goes right, it's a slice; if it goes left, it's a hook; if it goes straight, it's a miracle.

And did you ever hear of the sort of drive that golfers call a Rock Hudson? It's one that looks straight but turns out to be anything but.

It's just a theory

Although no one really knows why golf shots are named after birds, one theory is this:

In the 19th century 'bird' was American slang for 'good' or 'excellent', so a birdie was a good shot. Some say that it was first used when a player managed to go one under par for a hole he was playing, and the name stuck. The terms 'eagle' and 'albatross' were simply extensions of the bird theme, though one source claimed that the first person to go three under par was a certain Albert Ross. It has also been claimed that the sequence of birds becomes more exotic as the difficulty of the shot increases.

Lingo that has passed into the language

Not only does golf has its own specialist jargon, but some of the phrases have now gone into the language.

Par for the course
Now a handy all-purpose phrase meaning 'normal' or 'the usual state of affairs'. Strangely, you're now probably more likely to hear it off the golf course than on.

Bunkered
This means 'in a difficult situation' and one wonders whether it may in fact be a euphemism for a rather stronger word in every day use?

Golf widow
The 'er indoors, when he is outdoors on the golf course. The phrase has been adapted to other long-suffering spouses such as 'darts widows', 'snooker widows', 'Warcraft widows', etc. And although the women's game has been increasing in popularity over recent years we have not yet heard the phrase 'golf widower' – but it's only a matter of time.

Stymie
The origins of this word are far from clear, but for a long time it has meant a ball which is unplayable because an opponent's ball is in the way. The word is now in general usage for a situation in which someone has no possible options to get out of a tricky situation. Almost synonymous with a word from another game: 'snookered'.

(Put off your) Stroke
Being wrong-footed or distracted while doing something.

Tee off
Meaning of course to start off something. E.g. 'Let's tee off with minutes of the last meeting.' 'Teed off' has also been heard as a euphemism for 'peed off' though it does in the process lose its original golfing meaning.

Playing Through
Archie is about to tee off on the golf course when he feels a tap on his shoulder. He turns to find a man standing behind him who presents him with a card that says: 'I am a deaf mute. Please would you consider letting me play through.' Archie is taken aback at this impudence and crossly thrusts the card back in the deaf gentleman's hand. 'No. You cannot play through!' declares Archie. 'Your handicap gives you no such right!' Having made his position clear, Archie whacks his ball onto the green and walks away to finish the hole. A few moments later Archie is preparing sink his putt when he is a ball sails out of the sky, whacks him on the head and knocks him to the ground. The deaf mute comes striding over the green, up to Archie, and thrusts his hand in Archie's face, holding up four fingers.

And finally, possibly the
worst golf jokes in the world...

Q: What does a golfer do when he's hungry?
A: Stop for tee and a sand wedge.

Q: What's the difference between a rock star and a golfer?
A: Rock stars drive into swimming pools, golfers drive into lakes.

Q: What club should you use to get out of long grass?
A: The tufty club.

Q: How did the bad golfer hit two good balls?
A. He stood on a rake.

Two Mexican detectives are investigating the murder of Juan
Gonzalez.
  'How was he killed?' asks one detective.
  'With a golf gun,' replies the other.
  'A golf gun? What's a golf gun?'
  'I don't know, but it sure made a hole in Juan!'